NO HOLINESS, NO HEAVEN!

Antinomianism Today

RICHARD ALDERSON

THE BANNER OF TRUTH TRUST

THE BANNER OF TRUTH TRUST
3 Murrayfield Road, Edinburgh EH12 6EL
PO Box 621, Carlisle, Pennsylvania 17013, USA

★

© Richard Alderson 1986
First published 1986
Reprinted 2001
ISBN 085151 495 2

★

Scripture quotations in this publication
are from the Holy Bible, New International Version.
Copyright © 1973, 1978, International Bible Society

Typeset in 10/11/2 Linotron Plantin
At The Spartan Press Ltd, Lymington, Hants
Printed in Finland by WS Bookwell

Contents

1: *Paul's Divine Logic*

'Doesn't your Christian gospel teach morality?'

The questioner was an overseas doctor who had listened, rather impatiently, as I preached the gospel of justification by faith. I had explained that, even if we lead 'blameless' and 'upright' lives, all our morality and good works are 'filthy rags' in God's eyes. But when we abandon all hope of earning salvation and cast ourselves in simple faith on God's mercy, He accepts us for Christ's sake, washes us clean in His precious blood, and regards us as righteous in Him.

I was delighted that my questioner reacted as he did. It meant that I had been preaching the same gospel as that preached by the Apostle Paul. He argues at length in his Epistle to the Romans that man is vile; he is guilty before God; and he is helpless. At this point of self-despair, he is enabled to see that Christ alone can save him without works. So he comes as a pauper and is made rich by the grace of God in Christ Jesus. He comes unclean and is washed in the cleansing blood.

Augustus M. Toplady has caught Paul's theology to perfection:

> Nothing in my hand I bring,
> Simply to Thy cross I cling;
> Naked, come to Thee for dress;
> Helpless, look to Thee for grace;

> Foul, I to the fountain fly:
> Wash me, Saviour, or I die!

Does this mean that the very worst of men may go to heaven by trusting Another's righteousness? It does!

FURORE IN THE MORAL REALM

The Great Apostle is well aware of the moral furore his gospel must create. He proceeds to voice in theological terms the objection that had leapt to the mind of my questioner: 'What shall we say then? Shall we go on sinning, so that grace may increase?' Paul answers with a resounding 'By no means! We died to sin; how shall we live in it any longer?' Sin is unthinkable. To sin is to make merchandise of 'that wondrous cross on which the Prince of Glory died.' 'Don't you know that all of us who were baptised into Christ Jesus were baptised into his death? We were therefore buried with him through baptism into death in order that, just as Christ was raised from the dead through the glory of the Father, we too may live a new life.'

LIVE AS YOU PLEASE?

Unhappily, some have not followed Paul's divine logic. They have succumbed to the carnal reasoning described by Theodore Beza as 'the Devil's logic'. 'If you are justified by faith alone, you may live as you please. You have a place reserved in heaven, so sin to your heart's content!' This was the accusation the Church of Rome hurled in the face of Martin Luther when he preached justification by faith alone.

It is sadly true that some who are called evangelicals have fallen into error on this vital subject. And one does not hesitate to assert that the present state of the church – and the world – is closely related to this melancholy fact.

This book has been written to demonstrate the biblical truth that, while Christians are indeed justified by faith alone, they will inevitably demonstrate that faith by lives which are not merely moral but positively holy. Its thesis is well expressed in John Calvin's dictum: 'We are justified by faith alone – but the faith that justifies is never alone!' He meant, of course, that true saving faith is always accompanied by a holy life and by good works. Justification of necessity entails sanctification. In the words of the saintly Robert Murray McCheyne, 'If Christ justifies you, He will sanctify you! He will not save you and leave you in your sins.' Bishop Ryle puts it yet more succinctly: 'No holiness, no heaven!'

DEAD TO SIN

'Shall we go on sinning so that grace may increase?'

The problem raised by the Apostle Paul's question is what the man in the street would probably call 'lawlessness'. He would perhaps think in terms of disobedience to human laws and regulations of all kinds and his mind would conjure up pictures of football hooligans on the rampage, looters ransacking shops, militant strikers hurling what the Americans call 'rocks' at the police, and a host of other situations only too common in our day when so many do what is right in their own eyes.

The man in the street is reminded daily in the media of escalating crimes of violence, sexual offences, drug abuse and a host of other evils. What he might not suspect is that lawlessness goes much deeper than external acts of law-breaking and the erosion of ethical standards. It is, in fact, an entrenched atheistic philosophy intent on demolishing the divinely-decreed bases of life – the family, the forces of law and order (e.g. the police), the church, and the state itself.

LICENCE TO SIN?

The Apostle Paul, in writing Romans chapter six, may have had in mind the objections of some unnamed critic who had slanderously misconstrued God's grace in Christ as a licence to sin. Certainly some heretics later argued that the further they went into sin, the more glory God would get from rescuing them from degradation and shame. It is a view known to theologians and church historians as Antinomianism, a greek word meaning 'against law'. So 'lawlessness' is a pretty fair rendering in English. It also has the advantage of highlighting the word 'law'. The relationship of the Christian to the law of God soon became, and remains, the bone of contention in any discussion of Antinomianism.

It must be asserted at the outset that Antinomianism is not merely of historical interest, though its history is indeed fascinating. This view, with its attendant practices, is very much with us in the twentieth century. That is why this book has been written. It took shape during the course of very painful contact with this horrid perversion of God's truth and was fashioned in the furnace of affliction.

DEATH, SLAVERY AND MARRIAGE

Paul's most devastating exposure of Antinomianism is to be found in chapters 6 and 7 of his Epistle to the Romans, where he reduces to absurdity the claim that salvation by grace encourages sin.

Firstly, he argues that the Christian has died to sin once and for ever. He has therefore finished with it entirely. Christ has rescued him from its dominion and service. Risen with Christ, he now finds himself in a new realm of righteousness. In the new birth he has received a new life and a new nature which hates sin and loves holiness. For him to continue in sin is therefore a sheer impossibility. The Apostle John says exactly the same thing: 'No-one who is born of God will continue in sin, because God's seed remains in him; he cannot go on sinning because he has been born of God' (*I John 3:9*).

Holiness is now the general tenor of the Christian's life. Crucified, buried, quickened and risen with Christ, he walks in newness of life with Him. He lives his new life in the Spirit, a life which increasingly reflects Christ's own essential purity.

Secondly, Paul argues that Christians, once the slaves of Satan and of sin, are now the slaves of righteousness and of God. There is no middle way. Men are either enslaved to sin, which leads to death, or else they are Christ's bond-slaves and possessors of eternal life. Those who are sin's serfs thereby declare that they are not Christians at all.

Thirdly, Christians are now married to Christ. This glorious union brings forth the fruit of righteousness. It produces in the believer that likeness to Christ which is the essence of holiness.

From this it is evident that justification and sanctification, though distinct, are indivisible in practice. In the justified man the process of sanctification has of necessity already begun.

SIN COVERED AND SIN PURGED

The Antinomian error is a fatal confusion of justification with sanctification. This lies at the root of the problem. As we shall see, some think that justification by faith releases the Christian from the demands of the Moral Law. Others have asserted that since, in justification, God forgives all the believer's sins – past, present and future – sin is no longer a problem of any kind for the Christian. God, we are told, regards the believer as sinless. He is therefore free from all moral obligation expressed in terms of law.

This confusion is dispelled by a correct understanding of the distinction between the Christian's legal position before God and his actual condition in practice. Sanctification, it should be noted, has reference to the believer's experience. The man who is dead in transgressions and sins can do nothing to please God. But once God renews and justifies him, he is required to pursue sanctification with the whole of his ransomed being.

The distinctions between justification and sanctification may be characterised as follows. Justification is a legal act in which God the Judge absolves the believer from the guilt of sin and reckons to him the righteousness of Christ. It is therefore a matter of his status in the eyes of God's Law. But sanctification concerns a Christian's present subjective experience in this world. In sanctification his life is being changed to bring it into conformity to the will of the Lawgiver. In the one he is declared judicially righteous in Christ; in the other he is being made Christlike in character. In justification God imputes righteousness; in sanctification He imparts it. Justification is God's act done once and for all at conversion, while sanctification is a progressive work from conversion to glorification. Justification is therefore the same in all Christians, whereas sanctification varies in degree from Christian to Christian. Justification is objective because of what Christ has done *for* man, while sanctification is subjective and consists of what He now does *in* him. In the first the Christian is given the right or the title to heaven; in the second he is being made fit in his person for heaven. In justification his filthiness is covered; in sanctification that filthiness is being purged. The one restores him to God's favour; the other is restoring him to God's image.

These things are so united in the saving work of God that no true believer can stop at forgiveness and regard sanctification as a further step which is optional. It is totally foreign to Scripture to suggest that one can receive Christ as Saviour from hell, but not as the Lord who saves from sin. The Bible knows nothing of those who are 'Christians' but not yet 'disciples'; of 'believers' who are 'carnal' but not yet 'spiritual'; of those who are 'justified' but not yet 'sanctified'.

On the contrary, Scripture is full of warnings about those who make extravagant claims to fellowship with God but whose moral nature remains unchanged. They may have great charismatic gifts and engage in remarkable acts of philanthropy, yet still remain spiritually dead and strangers to grace (*I Cor. 13:1–3*). Those with true saving faith live as Christ lived. Those who persevere in a sinful life merely proclaim thereby that they are not Christians at all.

J. C. Ryle, in a comment upon the words of Christ, 'Blessed is that servant, whom his lord when he cometh shall find so doing' (*Luke 12:43*), shows the importance of the distinctions we have given above. He writes:

'It is not the servant who is found wishing and professing, but the servant who is found "doing," whom Jesus calls "blessed." The lesson is one which many, unhappily, shrink from giving, and many more shrink from receiving. We are gravely told that to talk of "working," and "doing," is legal, and brings Christians into bondage! Remarks of this kind should never move us. They savour of ignorance or perverseness. The lesson before us is not about justification, but about sanctification, – not about faith, but about holiness; the point is not *what a man should do to be saved*, – but *what ought a saved man to do*. The teaching of Scripture is clear and express upon this subject. A saved man ought to be "careful to maintain good works." (*Tit. 3:8.*) The desire of a true Christian ought to be, to be found "doing."[1]

[1] *Expository Thoughts on the Gospel of Luke*, vol. 2, p. 90.

2: 'A Blasphemous Impiety'

Readers will appreciate that the following brief review of historical Antinomianism is not introduced out of mere antiquarian interest but out of the conviction that much can be learnt from history that is of very practical application in our own day.

This brief overview should serve the twofold purpose of informing the mind and warning us against the very real dangers of what Luther in his day called 'a blasphemous impiety'. And if we are tempted to think that Luther is outdated, let us remember that Dr Martyn Lloyd-Jones has warned his twentieth-century contemporaries of the prevalence of what he termed 'one of the most subtle, dangerous heresies'.[2]

We have seen the Apostle Paul's out-and-out rejection of Antinomianism in his Epistle to the Romans. Other broadsides against lawlessness throughout the New Testament provide ample proof that a Christian profession severed from holiness was already a serious problem in the early church. Paul warns the Philippians of those 'whose God is their stomach and their glory is in their shame. Their mind is on earthly things'. He cautions the Corinthians against an Antinomian attitude to incest. John warns against idolatry and fornication. Peter and Jude both pen searing attacks on carnal teachers who bring damnable heresies into the church – 'godless men, who

[2]Lloyd-Jones, D. M. *Darkness and Light: An Exposition of Ephesians 4:17–5:17* (1982), p. 348, Banner of Truth.

change the grace of our God into a licence for immorality . . . pollute their own bodies . . . foam up their shame . . . follow after their own evil desires.' James warns those whose 'faith' does not produce works that their faith is, to say the least, suspect.

EARLY ANTINOMIANISM

A brief review of the history of Antinomianism will give some impression of the better-known appearances of this heresy, which has surfaced in many different forms over the running centuries.

An early sect of professing Christians known as Cainites regarded Cain, Esau, Korah, the Sodomites, Judas and other reprobates as the real heroes of the faith! Carpocrates turned morality on its head by teaching that every vice is really a virtue to be indulged to one's heart's content. Some argued that, as mud cannot damage gold, so sin could not stain their essential nature. They were therefore free to sin without any scruple.

Marcion in the second century foreshadowed a later brand of Antinomianism when he drove an absolute wedge between law and gospel in a scathing attack on the law of Moses. He was an early higher critic, 'editing with a penknife' the parts of Scripture he did not like. Antinomianism is still wielding a scalpel to excise God's moral law from the written Word.

Throughout the Middle Ages, charges of the most gross immorality were brought against various groups. At this distance in time, it is impossible to distinguish fact from fiction. Under torture, people may confess to crimes of which they are certainly not guilty. And one must remember that the persecutors have written all the books! Nevertheless, if the contemporary accounts are to be credited, there were those in mediaeval times who considered themselves sinless by virtue of their union with the Godhead, and they argued that this left them free to indulge their vices. No sin, they said, can be imputed to those 'made perfect in love', to those so totally one with God that even an angel cannot tell the difference between them. The later Middle Ages appear to have spawned a widespread Antinomianism of this type.

ANTINOMIANISM IN THE REFORMATION ERA

The Reformation era saw the rise of sects such as the Libertines, who made the familiar plea that, as spiritual men free from the law, they were at liberty to give free rein to all their desires. They came under Calvin's censure.

Luther, for his part, crossed swords with Johann Agricola, 'the Father of Modern Antinomianism'. Agricola rejected the Mosaic Law in its entirety. He claimed that the gospel alone, not the law, could bring men to repentance. So the law could be relegated to limbo since it had no more relevance for the Christian than it had for the unsaved. Even the Ten Commandments were no rule of life for the believer. And that, retorted Luther in righteous anger, was a 'blasphemous impiety'.

Others were quick to seize on, and add to, Agricola's errors. The law, they asserted, was not worthy to be called the Word of God, and all who preached it were demon-possessed. To preach holiness and chastity was to prostitute the gospel, since all who believed were in the way of salvation, even though they were adulterers, villains, prostitutes or sinners of any description. History bears grim testimony to the fearful aftermath of the teaching of such perverted doctrines. Those interested may read the story, for instance, of the Antinomian branch of the Anabaptists with its catalogue of debauchery and violence.

Great Britain did not escape the ravages of Antinomianism. The more than doubtful 'privilege' of first propagating this doctrinal aberration in England in the seventeenth century belongs to John Eaton, now called 'the Father of English Antinomianism'. As always, there were those who were only too anxious to perpetuate and embellish error. They insisted that the law was useless to Christians, either as a rule of life or as a means of self-examination. Seizing on the acknowledged fact that the law supplies no power to fulfil its demands, one Antinomian preacher cried, 'Away with the law, which cuts off a man's legs and then bids him walk'.[3] This was an ill-conceived attack. The same charge could be preferred against the gospel, which goes further and commands the dead to live! Only the Holy Spirit can give life and power to law or gospel. And when He does, He enables the gospel believer to keep the law of God.

'PRACTISING' AND 'THEORETICAL'

The worst type of Antinomianism was seen in the Ranters, 'who by their enthusiastic propaganda seduced multitudes from the fellowship of the evangelical denominations' (A. H. Newman).[4] Some of these fanatics claimed that they were God. Christ, they said, was a deceiver; there was no devil, no heaven, no hell; prayer was useless; preaching, like the Bible, was a pack of lies. Their lives certainly matched the evil of these blasphemous propositions. It is good to be able to record that Arminians and Calvinists were (and are) united in their opposition to this ugly teaching.

[3]Quoted in Pagitt, Ephraim. *Heresiography, or a Description of Hereticks* (1645), p. 90. (London).

[4]Newman, A. H. in *The New Schaff-Herzog Encyclopedia of Religious Knowledge* (1908), ed. Jackson, vol. I, p. 198. Funk & Wagnalls.

It must be said, in fairness, that there have always been two principal types of Antinomian. Those like the Ranters, whose lives were immoral, were 'practical' (i.e. 'practising') Antinomians. Such were often coarse ignoramuses, who despised scholarship and culture as diabolical. Others – of whom there were many – were 'doctrinal' (i.e. 'theoretical') Antinomians, and their lives were above reproach. Among such we may number Dr Tobias Crisp, an erudite and sophisticated theologian. Nevertheless, it is a sheer fact of history that theoretical Antinomianism tends in time to become practical.

NEW WORLD

The 'high priestess' of Antinomianism in the New World was Mrs Anne Hutchinson. She caused great havoc and division in the churches of New England by accusing ministers of preaching a 'covenant of works' rather than a 'covenant of grace'. In the strong language of the day – used freely by both sides in the controversy – all such were described as 'antichrists'. Her critics responded in kind by dubbing her 'the American Jezebel'.

Among other Antinomian tenets, Mrs Hutchinson stressed her own brand of assurance of salvation. This was always given immediately by the Spirit, not through the Word of God, and was never to be doubted. Furthermore, she believed that it was 'soul-damning error' to make sanctification an evidence of justification. A Christian, she seemed to teach, never became inherently holy in himself, since all his sanctification was in Christ. So, provided he 'believed' in Christ, he must never be concerned about his personal sins – that would mean he was under a covenant of works.

OLD WORLD

To return to the Old World, Antinomianism invaded the Strict Baptist churches of England towards the end of the eighteenth century. The Hyper-Calvinism that virtually made God the author of evil and denied human responsibility brought in its train the Antinomian rejection of the moral law as a rule of life. Robert Hall spoke at the time of 'that thick-skinned monster of the ooze and mire, making rapid strides through the land, convulsing and disorganizing so many of our [Baptist] churches'.[5] At the same period the dying Rowland Hill declared, 'The greatest curse that ever entered the Church of God is dirty Antinomianism'.[6]

In the nineteenth century, Antinomianism received a further fillip from an unexpected direction – J. N. Darby, founder of Exclusive Brethrenism and father of modern dispensationalism with its disparagement of law over against grace. 'Oh, how I hate that law!' said one dispensationalist. And Professor Chafer added, 'The law adds nothing to grace but confusion and contradiction.' Thanks to the Scofield Bible, this view is now tragically accepted as orthodox by many.

The 'evil of gigantic size and deadly malignity' of which Robert Hall wrote has become 'the epidemic malady' of the twentieth century. Arthur Pink described it as 'the popular belief of our day'.[7] Since Pink's death in 1952, we have witnessed the rise of movements like the New Morality (which has proved to be the Old Immorality in disguise) and Situational Ethics, with their stress on 'love'

---

[5]Hall, Robert. Quoted in *Dictionary of Christian Churches and Sects* (1856), ed. Marsden, p. 56. Richard Bentley.

[6]Quoted in Morrison, John, *The Fathers and Founders of the London Missionary Society*, vol. 2, p. 168.

[7]Pink, Arthur W. *The Law and the Saint* (n.d.), p. 13. Evangelical Press.

as the sole criterion of truth. They have their (false) prophets of love whose favourite texts are I John 4:8 ('God is love') and Romans 13:8 ('Love one another; for he who loves his fellow-man has fulfilled the law').

Putting love in opposition to law, they reject the objective law of God in favour of their own subjective impressions of what is right. They soon discover that 'love' can condone virtually any sin. Instead of fulfilling the law, they are unashamedly breaking it – witness the flagrant immorality of the notorious Moses David and his Family of Love, the so-called 'Children of God'. 'God's only law is love,' says this practising Antinomian. 'I don't have to keep the Ten Commandments! All I have to do is love and do whatever I do in love.'[8]

This has had a devastating effect on the church as well as the world, so that the situation is now very critical. It is the bounden duty of every Christian to resist with might and main the evils of this latter-day Antinomianism.

MISINTERPRETING LAW

Antinomianism is thus essentially an attack on God's law –and a very misguided attack at that. We must therefore examine its failure to understand the biblical teaching on this vital subject. We believe that it is precisely because of their misinterpretation of the law that Antinomians have failed to understand the biblical doctrines of human sin and guilt, repentance, faith, justification, sanctification and assurance.

As we discuss some of these topics in more detail in the chapters which follow, their relationship to Antinomianism will emerge.

[8]Moses, David. Quoted in Davis, Deborah. *The Children of God* (1984), p. 190. Marshalls.

3: *Law: Civic, Ceremonial and Moral*

The term 'Antinomian' was coined by Martin Luther from the Greek word meaning 'against law'. He used it of those who thought that with the coming of the Christian gospel, God's law could now be safely relegated to oblivion. There is a sense in which this heresy arose from a misunderstanding of the Apostle John's statement, 'The law was given by Moses, but grace and truth came by Jesus Christ' (*John 1:17, AV*). This was interpreted to mean that Moses and his law have now been superseded by Jesus Christ and His grace. Other statements about Christians not being 'under law' but 'under grace' lent weight to this view. The fact that there is no 'but' in the Greek original of John 1:17 should have given the Antinomians pause, quite apart from many other New Testament statements which establish the moral law as an essential element in the life of grace.

As we shall see, there is law in the life of grace just as there was grace in the giving of the law. Indeed the law is so much a part of the Christian life that John insists that those who do not keep God's law have no reason to suppose that they are Christians at all. Says John, 'The man who says, "I know him," but does not do what he commands is a liar, and the truth is not in him' (*I John 2:4*). In the words of Dr Lloyd-Jones, 'If the "grace" you have received does not help you to keep the law, you have not received grace'.[9] As we shall see, this thesis is developed at great length in the New Testament by all the inspired writers.

'TO THE GALLOWS WITH MOSES!'

The apparent conflict between law and grace, law and gospel, faith and works was raised in acute form at the time of the Reformation, when Luther introduced his term 'Antinomian'. It was directed against Johann Agricola, High Priest of modern Antinomianism, who took a very radical stance and placed an unbridgeable gulf between law and gospel. 'It is better', he asserted, 'for Christians to know nothing about the law; evangelical preachers should preach the pure gospel and no law; Christians by good works are of the Devil'.[10] In the intemperate language all too common in theological controversy, he thundered, 'The Ten Commandments belong to the law courts, not in the pulpit . . . To the gallows with Moses!'[11] This aroused the wrath of Martin Luther, who proceeded to hang Agricola – or at least his heretical views – on the gallows erected by the New Testament for those who reject God's holy law.

If it is true that Antinomians are 'against law', we must first ask what is meant by 'law'. Any student of the Old Testament soon realises that the word is used with very different connotations. There are, in fact, three basic categories of law, traditionally known as civic, ceremonial, and moral.

[9]Lloyd-Jones, D. Martyn. *Studies in the Sermon on the Mount* (1959), vol. I, p. 197. Inter-Varsity Fellowship.
[10]Agricola, Johann. Quoted in *The Protestant Theological and Ecclesiastical Encyclopaedia* (1856), ed. Bomberger, vol. I, p. 180. T. & T. Clark.
[11]Agricola, Johann. Quoted in *The New Encyclopaedia Britannica: Micropaedia*, vol. 1, p. 144.

CIVIC LAW

As regards the civic law, it is clear that Israel was originally a theocracy – ruled by God, who communicated His will directly to prophets like Moses. In this way, a large body of legislation was laid down, governing such matters as murder, theft, immorality and, in fact, misdemeanours of all kinds. The Israelite state had divine sanction to impose every type of punishment from the death penalty downwards. As God's plenipotentiaries, they were often punishing not so much 'crime' as 'sin'.

Has the Israelite civic law passed away? It is clear that the answer must be 'yes' for it was bound up with the Old Testament economy. Our Lord announced the demise of theocracy when the kingdom passed from Israel to the church. 'The kingdom of God', said Jesus to the Jews, 'will be taken away from you and given to a people who will produce its fruit' (*Matt. 21:43*). That 'people' is the church which is to be found among all nations. The Mosaic civic law belonged in its binding authority to the period when one nation was ruled by God as its immediate head and judge.

Any attempt to reinstate theocratic rule – and there have been many – must therefore be adjudged misconceived. This applies equally to Calvin's Geneva and the Puritan experiment in New England. A militant Islam is attempting in our day to impose 'theocratic' control in some countries – with capital punishment for adultery and amputation for theft. This is a far more terrible error than any temporary Christian attempts at theocracy.

CEREMONIAL LAW

What of the ceremonial law? Is it still in force? The New Testament is much more explicit about this. Christ came to fulfil it in every detail. He was the Antitype of all the types and shadows of the ceremonial law – the tabernacle and temple with their furnishings and especially their sacrificial offerings. By one sacrifice for sins for ever, our Great High Priest has done away with the need for the ceremonial law – as we shall see in detail later.

The attempt by Christian converts from Pharisaism to impose on Gentile Christians the intolerable yoke of Old Testament ceremonial law was decisively defeated at the Council of Jerusalem (*Acts 15*). This was legalism. The Colossian converts were charged by the Great Apostle not to submit to such legalistic bondage as regulations about food, drink, religious festivals, the new moon and the sabbath (*Col. 2:16*). Christians are not bound by that kind of law.

And we in our day need to resist attempts by latter-day legalists to enslave us by man-made regulations and shibboleths. These self-appointed popes assure us that God has revealed to them His displeasure with those Christians who possess a television set, keep pets, read for university degrees, associate with believers outside their own party – the list is endless. The Apostle Paul has already answered all such impositions: 'Do not let yourselves be burdened again by a yoke of slavery' (*Gal. 5:1*).

MORAL LAW

All modern works of reference, both Christian and secular, agree in defining Antinomianism as the view that the Moral Law (the 10 Commandments) is not binding on Christians as a rule of life. In the words of one of its modern spokesmen, Professor Sperry Chafer, who espouses this position: 'No Christian is under the law as a rule of life'.[12] We here present the biblical view – that the

---

[12]Chafer, Lewis Sperry. *He that is Spiritual* (1967), p. 64. Zondervan.

Moral Law, spiritually understood, is God's blueprint for Christian living.

In the first place, the Moral Law reflects God's own essential attributes. As God is spiritual, so is His Law. Since God is holy, His Law is also holy (*Rom. 7:12,14*). As God cannot change, it follows that His Law cannot change. It has eternal validity and can never be abrogated.

God the Creator has imposed His Law on all created beings – angels and men alike – as the objective expression of His will (*Psa. 103:20; Rom. 2:15*). As Moral Governor of the universe, He is entitled to the unquestioning obedience of all His creatures.

Obedience to God (because He is Creator) and to His Moral Law (because it reflects His sovereign will) lies at the heart of all true religion – and thus of sanctification. Becoming a Christian does not alter the fact that I am still a created being under obligation to obey. What conversion does is to enable me to render to God that obedience of which I was incapable as an unbeliever. What is more, it grants me an over-riding desire to obey, since God is now also my Redeemer in Christ Jesus.

It is clear that God imposed His Moral Law on man from the very beginning. Adam and Eve suffered for breaking it, as did Cain. That Law was written on the hearts of all men (*Rom. 2:14–15*). It was re-instituted in the time of Moses in order to define and condemn sin (*Rom. 4:15; 5:13*). John actually describes sin as 'lawlessness' or 'the transgression of the law' (*I John 3:4*). To be saved from sin therefore means to be saved from transgressing the law – and thus enabled to keep it.[13]

The Ten Commandments were explicitly applied to God's redeemed people (*Exod. 20:1–17*). Antinomians have argued that, with the advent of the New Covenant,

[13]See, e.g., Macleod, Donald in *Living the Christian Life* (1974), pp. 5ff. Westminster Conference Report.

those commandments lapsed. But this is patently untrue. Our Lord Himself asserted their perpetual validity: 'Do not think that I have come to abolish the law or the prophets; I have not come to abolish them, but to fulfil them. For I tell you the truth, until heaven and earth disappear, not the smallest letter, not the least stroke of a pen, will by any means disappear from the law until everything is accomplished' (*Matt. 5:17–18*). He then issued a very solemn warning against becoming Antinomian and commended those who practise and teach the law: 'Anyone who breaks one of the least of these commandments and teaches others to do the same will be called least in the kingdom of heaven, but whoever practises and teaches these commands will be called great in the kingdom of heaven' (*Matt. 5:19*).

What Christ did was to rid the commandments of the misinterpretations of the Pharisees. Dr Kevan points out that our Lord did not say 'unless your righteousness surpasses that of Moses' but 'that of the Pharisees' (*Matt. 5:20*).[14] Christ proceeded to show the essential spirituality of the law. It is concerned primarily with men's motives, and not merely with their actions. So when God said, 'You shall not murder,' there was also included its source – unrighteous anger. And when He said, 'You shall not commit adultery,' the command also prohibited all lustful thoughts. These things exposed men to the condemnation of God and they still do!

THE ROYAL LAW

James urges on his Christian readers the need to obey the law. 'If you really keep the royal law found in Scripture, "Love your neighbour as yourself", you are doing right'

---

[14]Kevan, Ernest F. *The Moral Law* (1963), p. 71 Sovereign Grace Publishers, U.S.A.

(*Jas. 2:8*). The Royal Law is in fact the Moral Law given to Moses by God in Leviticus 19:18, which James quotes. The 'law' which the apostle warns his readers not to break, and which he calls 'the law of liberty', is nothing other than the Ten Commandments (*Jas. 2:11–12*). For the Christian, obedience and liberty belong together, the requirements of the Moral Law being exactly suited to his moral nature.

Paul makes no apology for imposing the Fifth Commandment on his Ephesian readers: 'Children, obey your parents in the Lord, for this is right. Honour your father and mother – which is the first commandment with a promise – that it may go well with you and that you may enjoy long life on the earth' (*Eph. 6:1–3*).

Even where the New Testament does not explicitly quote the law of the Ten Commandments, it everywhere reflects its exact prohibitions. Like their Old Testament counterparts, New Testament believers are exhorted not to worship idols, or misuse God's name, or murder, or commit adultery, or steal, or give false testimony, or covet. Gospels and epistles alike are replete with other commands also addressed to God's people – to give, to pray, to fight, to work, to love, to obey, to resist Satan and his temptations – and a host of other such things. These exhortations are all the law of Christ for Christians – and they are to be obeyed. Paul, the apostle of grace, puts it quite bluntly: 'Circumcision is nothing and uncircumcision is nothing. Keeping God's commands is what counts' (*I Cor. 7:19*).

Paul explicitly denies that he is 'free from God's law'. He asserts positively that he is 'under Christ's law' (*I Cor. 9:21*). The Greek literally reads 'in the law (or 'in-lawed') to Christ'. So as 'Christ's law-abiding one', he is 'under the law's authority and teaching'. It is the sinful Antinomian mind that hates God and refuses to submit to His Law

(*Rom. 8:7*). The Christian has a renewed mind that delights in that Law and is, in fact, its willing slave (*Rom. 7:22,25*). He has the mind of Christ – and Christ loved and obeyed His Father's Law (*Psa. 40:8*). Those who are Christlike must therefore of necessity love and obey that Law also (*I John 5:3*). Indeed, the Holy Spirit writes it in the minds and hearts of all God's children (*Heb. 8:10*). He would scarcely do so if it were no longer binding on Christians! In fact we know that the Father's very purpose in sending the Son to die for sin was 'that the righteous requirements of the law might be fully met in us (Christians)' (*Rom. 8:4*).

On this subject Octavius Winslow speaks as follows to fellow Christians:

'Saints of God, keep the eye of your faith intently and immoveably fixed upon Christ, your sole pattern. Our Lord did not keep that law that his people might be lawless. He did not honour that law that they might dishonour its precepts. His obedience provided no licence for our disobedience. His fulfilment releases us not from the obligation, – the sweet and pleasant, yet solemn obligation – to holiness of life. Our faith does not make void the law, but rather establishes the law. The "righteousness of the law is fulfilled in us" when we "walk after the Spirit," in lowly conformity to Christ's example. Was he meek and lowly in heart? Did he bless when cursed? Did he, when reviled, revile not again? Did he walk in secret with God? Did he always seek to do those things which pleased his Father? Did he live a life of faith, and prayer, and toil? So let us imitate him, that of us it may be said, "These are they who *follow the Lamb* whithersoever he goeth."'[15]

[15]Winslow, Octavius, *No Condemnation in Christ Jesus*, As unfolded in Romans Chapter 8, 1853, pp. 50–51.

Such words were once the universally accepted conviction of those who taught historic Christianity, but they have been challenged again in England in recent times. The Rev Michael Eaton, for example, is one who sees no need for Christians to honour the law. He writes, 'Christians are in no way under this tyrannical figure, the law.'[16] Agricola, he added, had got it right, but unfortunately as Agricola did not have the kudos of Luther, his view was squashed! Dr R. T. Kendall, who published Mr Eaton's article and who claims to be the source of his views, writes in similar vein. He complains that, when he preaches that Christians 'are not under the law and don't need the Ten Commandments, some people panic and become hysterical.'[17]

John Calvin certainly remained perfectly calm. Familiar as he was with the views of 'that arch-Antinomian, Agricola', he wrote, 'Certain ignorant persons rashly cast out the whole of Moses and bid farewell to the two Tables of the Law . . . Let us banish this wicked thought from our minds.'[18] Professor John Murray concurs: 'In the denial of the permanent authority and sanctity of the Moral Law there is a direct thrust at the very centre of our holy faith, for it is a thrust at the veracity and authority of our Lord Himself'.[19]

GENUINE DIFFICULTIES

One can sympathise with those sincere Christians who have been misled regarding the place of Law in the

[16]Eaton, Michael in *Westminster Record* (Oct. 1984), Westminster Chapel, London, p. 14.

[17]Kendall, R. T. in *Westminster Chapel News* (Apr/June 1984), p. 3.

[18]Calvin, John. *Institutes of the Christian Religion* (1961), vol. I, p. 361. Student Christian Movement.

[19]*Collected Writings of John Murray* (1976), vol. 1, p. 202. Banner of Truth.

believer's life. They may have been taught that, since Christians are justified by faith alone without the deeds of the Law, then works can have no place in the Christian life. They may have been led to think that obedience to the Moral Law is sheer legalism – justification by works.

Some such Christians may have been terrified by a law which thundered its terrors and condemnation from Sinai. Then, once they have found refuge in Christ from the curse of the Law, they may wrongly feel that they are still to regard the law as their enemy. And they may suppose that they find support for this attitude in verses which declare that they are 'not under law' and are 'dead to the law'.

Confusion sometimes arises because of a failure to realise that these verses are dealing with justification. Thus, when a verse like Romans 6:14 asserts that Christians are 'not under law but under grace', the writer means that Christians are not required to keep the Law in order to obtain justification. Since it is a spiritual impossibility to justify ourselves by works, we must be justified by grace through faith alone. If any obedience of our own rendered to the law could justify, then Christ died in vain (*Gal. 2:21*). The Law *cannot* justify, but the fault lies not in the Law, which is holy, but in man's sin (*Rom. 7:7–14*).

Galatians 3:13 asserts that 'Christ redeemed us from the curse of the law'. This has been interpreted to mean that the Law can do nothing but curse. But here again, Paul is dealing with justification. Certainly, the Law pronounces a curse on all who are misguided enough to seek justification by their own works. Those under conviction of sin view the Law as a cruel tyrant and taskmaster threatening eternal punishment for failure to do the impossible. But the converted man sees the curse as a blessing in disguise, for it drove him to the Christ who bore that curse for him. Again, this is no reflection on the Law as such. It is from

[25]

the curse of the Law that we are redeemed, not from the Law itself.

When Romans 7:14 says that we died to the Law, it does not mean that the Law died. It is we who died to the Law – the Law is very much alive! The change that occurs is not in the Law but in us. Raised with Christ to new life, we now love the same Law which once we hated. It is a sign of true conversion when a man's heart is melted to love God's eternal Law and when his will is bent to obey it.

4: *Wedges*

Antinomians have sometimes attempted to avoid the thrust of Scripture by asserting that they *are* under the law – but the law that they are under is the Law of Christ, not the Law of God! We must examine further this extraordinary attempt to drive a wedge between Father and Son.

MORAL LAW V. LAW OF CHRIST?

Modern Antinomians are drawing a totally false distinction between the Ten Commandments, which are said to produce 'mere morality', and the Law of Christ, which produces holiness. Listen to Dr R. T. Kendall expounding this view: 'The Moral Law is not the Christian's code of conduct, for true godliness is never to be achieved by being under the Moral Law. It will make you a legalist – long-faced, grouchy, without joy or peace'.[20]

The same author tells us that some Jewish Christians had 'sunk so low and degenerated so far' that James had to quote the Ten Commandments to them – 'something he ought not to have to do'! After this misinterpretation of James, he proceeds to enlist the Apostle Paul in his cause. To this end, he quotes Romans 3:28 –, 'Therefore we conclude that a man is justified by faith without the deeds of the law'. 'What Paul meant,' we are told, 'was that the

[20]Kendall, R. T. *Antinomianism Exposed* (Sermon, 12/10/1980). Westminster Chapel cassette.

Moral Law has no place in Christian experience'! But Paul meant no such thing. This is the typical Antinomian confusion of justification with sanctification.[21] Dr Kendall senses some difficulty, for to be 'without law' means that one is Antinomian. So he hastens to add, 'That doesn't mean that the law has no place. We as Christians are not under the Moral Law, but we *are* under the Law of Christ.'

Dr Kendall then proceeds to claim that the Law of Christ is 'a much higher law than the Moral Law, far more demanding. It presents a far greater challenge than the Moral Law, which is really the easy way out. It's just so easy to keep the Moral Law and hate the Law of Christ.' Has the writer of these words never read the Sermon on the Mount where we have Christ's summary of the Moral Law as perfect love to God and man? Who ever found that 'so easy'?

We must answer this view further. There can be no dichotomy between Father and Son. The Father's Moral Law *is* the Law of Christ the Son. This ought to need no demonstration. It is the law of love which is laid down by both James and Paul: 'Love your neighbour as yourself'. They are quoting Leviticus 19:18 and it is the heart of the Moral Law! How can the New Testament law be 'much higher' when it goes no further than quoting and explaining the Old Testament Law? The suggestion of some other and higher law is entirely without foundation. It was the Moral Law, already in existence, of which Christ said that He came not to destroy but to fulfil it (*Matt. 5:17*).

LAW V. LOVE?

There is, however, a further fallacy attaching to Antinomian reasoning. If we have love, they argue, we do not need

---

[21]Dr Kendall's confusion is very evident in his 'Antinomianism and the Law' in *Westminster Record* (March 1985), pp. 14ff.

any external law to guide us. But the Moral Law is not external to the Christian. God's promise in the new covenant was to put His Law in the mind and write it on the heart (*Jer. 31:33*). So Paul says of the Corinthian Christians, 'You show that you are a letter from Christ, the result of our ministry, written not with ink but with the Spirit of the living God; not on tablets of stone, but on tablets of human hearts' (*2 Cor. 3:3*). So we can agree with Thomas Manton that if the Spirit has engraved God's Moral Law so legibly on our hearts, Christ is not going to erase it.[22] That, we might add, would be to drive a wedge between Spirit and Son.

Antinomians certainly drive a wedge between love and law, as if they were mutually incompatible. Gerald Coates writes, 'When the believer properly fulfils the royal law of love for God and neighbour, he renders the law obsolete.'[23] But there is no essential conflict. They 'belong inseparably together,' as J. I. Packer tells us: 'Law is needed as love's eyes; love is needed as law's heartbeat. Law without love is Pharisaism; love without law is Antinomianism.'[24] Samuel Bolton agrees: 'Without law, love is blind.' In fact, the Apostle Paul shows us the eyes needed by love. Those eyes are the Ten Commandments and he shows how the highest form of love is inherent in the very meaning of the Commandments: 'He who loves his fellow-man has fulfilled the law. The commandments, "Do not commit adultery", "Do not murder", "Do not steal", "Do not covet", and whatever other commandment there may be, are summed up in this one rule: "Love your neighbour as your-

[22]Quoted in Kevan, Ernest F. *The Grace of Law: A Study in Puritan Theology* (1964), p. 157. Carey Kingsgate.
[23]Coates, Gerald. *What on Earth is this Kingdom?* (1983), p. 71. Kingsway.
[24]Packer, J. I. *God has spoken: Revelation and the Bible* (1979), p. 130. Hodder & Stoughton.

self"' (*Rom. 13: 8–10*).

So when Paul says that 'he who loves his fellow-man has fulfilled the law,' he means that love is essentially obedience to the law. In Theodore Beza's words, 'Love is not perfected, except as the fulfilling of the law.' The Apostle John says exactly the same thing: 'This is love: that we walk in obedience to his commands' (*2 John 6*). Scripture instinctively thinks of love, not as mere feeling, but in terms of loving action. 'God so loved the world that he gave his one and only Son', says John 3:16 (the verse described by Martin Luther as 'the gospel in a nutshell'). And we must show our love in action – the action explicitly prescribed by God's holy law. 'Carry each other's burdens,' says Paul, 'and in this way you will fulfil the law of Christ' (*Gal. 6:2*). Our Lord Himself said: 'If you love me, you will obey what I command' (*John 14:15*).

We can but agree with John Wesley, who wrote, 'Keep close to the law if thou wilt keep close to Christ.' In the words which were so often on the lips of Dr Lloyd-Jones, 'Holiness is not an experience you have; holiness is keeping the law of God.'

WHY LAW?

In his Epistle to the Galatians, Paul asks what purpose was served by the giving of the law, and he answers his own question. 'It was added because of transgressions' (*Gal. 3:19*). This means that one purpose that God had in giving the law – it was certainly not His only purpose – was to keep sin in bounds. Not that the law is essentially negative. We have our Lord's own authority for asserting that the law is primarily positive and may be summarised as love to God and to man. Nevertheless, the Ten Commandments do contain negative elements and those were intended to restrain sin and crime. Men were – and still are – commanded not to worship false gods, nor kill, nor steal, nor commit adultery, nor do anything else that makes life a hell on earth. The promulgation of laws certainly can have a deterrent effect, as every government knows.

PREACHING LAW

The question at once arises, should the law of God be preached evangelistically to sinners from Christian pulpits? Some Antinomians have said – and still say – 'no!'. The Apostle Paul thought otherwise. The classic passage on this point is the first part of the Epistle to the Romans. (It is the passage used by Luther in his reply to Agricola, entitled *Against the Antinomians*, 1539). In essence, Paul is demonstrating that man is a sinner who has broken God's holy law. He is therefore guilty and under judgment.

The depth of man's depravity is painfully evident in the list of vices the apostle adduces in Romans chapter one. Anyone unconvinced will find further evidence in chapters two and three, and many other passages could be adduced to the same effect.

The Apostle's case is that one function of the law is to reveal sin. 'Through the law', he says, 'we become conscious of sin' (*Rom. 3:20*). As he adds later in the Epistle, 'I would not have known what sin was except through the law. For I would not have known what coveting really was if the law had not said, "Do not covet"' (*Rom. 7:7*).

It is the law alone that exposes sin for what it is. Ignorance of the law therefore spells ignorance of sin. And ignorance of sin spells damnation. For salvation is salvation from sin. How can I experience salvation from that of which I am ignorant? These verses are sufficient in and of themselves to silence Antinomian quibbles regarding the use of the law in evangelism.

But the law actually does more than simply expose sin – it throws it into greater relief. This is partly what the apostle means by saying that 'the law was added so that the trespass might increase' (*Rom. 5:20*). Man begins to see how offensive sin is – 'that through the commandment sin might become utterly sinful' (*Rom. 7:13*).

All this leads to a conviction that the sinner is guilty before God. 'Now we know that whatever the law says, it says to those who are under the law, so that every mouth may be silenced and the whole world held accountable to God' (*Rom. 3:19*).

We observe here that it was the giving of the law that enabled God to impute to man the guilt of sin. 'For before the law was given, sin was in the world. But sin is not taken into account when there is no law' (*Rom. 5:13*). And with guilt came wrath. Now that the law has come, 'The wrath of God is being revealed from heaven against all godlessness and wickedness of men who suppress the truth by their wickedness' (*Rom. 1:18*). Again we note that it is the law that calls forth God's wrath – 'Because the law brings wrath; and where there is no law there is no transgression' (*Rom. 4:15*).

The apostle thus vindicates to the hilt his case for preaching the law to man.

LAW WORK

It is a simple fact that all the great gospel preachers of the Protestant era have employed what they called a 'law work' in their evangelism. They first laid down the law as the foundation on which to build the gospel. They argued, with Scripture, that men needed to feel the enormity of their sin before they would feel constrained to seek relief for that sin in the gospel.

Our blessed Lord used a medical illustration in defending His use of this method. 'It is not the healthy,' He asserted, 'who need a doctor, but the sick. But go and learn what this means: "I desire mercy and not sacrifice." For I have not come to call the righteous, but sinners to repentance' (*Matt. 9:12–13*). It is the sick, not the healthy, who go to the doctor. And it is 'sinners', not the 'righteous', who fly to Christ for spiritual healing.

CONVICTION BEFORE CONVERSION

This spiritual truth is sometimes put in terms of the dictum, 'Conviction comes before conversion'. This could be illustrated at great length. Luther, for example, wrote: 'I have followed the rule not to minister comfort to any person except to those who have become contrite and are sorrowing because of their sin – those who have despaired of self-help, whom the law has terrified like a leviathan that has pounced upon them and almost perplexed them. For these are the people for whose sake Christ came into the world and He will not have a smoking flax to be quenched (*Isa. 42:3*).'[25]

Robert Bolton stated it in terms of 'first wounding by the law, and then healing by the gospel'.[26] Another old Puritan divine employed the homely illustration, 'The scarlet thread of the gospel is attached to the sharp needle of the law'. Nearer our own day, J. C. Ryle has said, 'The beginning of the way to heaven is to feel that we are on the way to hell'. That is conviction of sin – and it comes through the law.

While man can rely on his own resources, he will do so. Only when he is desperate will he apply for mercy. In the

---

[25]Luther, Martin. *Lectures on Genesis*. Quoted in Walther, C. F. W. *The Proper Distinction between Law and Gospel* (1928), p. 98. Concordia.

[26]Bolton, Robert. Quoted in Kevan, Ernest F. *The Grace of Law* (1964), p. 91. Carey Kingsgate.

words of J. N. Darby, 'When the Prodigal son was hungry, he went to feed upon husks – but when he was starving, he turned to his father!' He was one of the 'weary and heavy laden' to whom the gospel call comes:

> Come, ye weary, heavy-laden,
> Bruised and broken by the fall;
> If you tarry till you're better,
> You will never come at all!
> Not the righteous –
> Sinners Jesus came to call!

(Joseph Hart)

As we have seen, the law is God's appointed instrument to bring a man under conviction of sin. Until that time, man is content to think in terms of mere externals. Like the Pharisees, he can easily satisfy himself that he can please God and meet His requirements. He can justify himself by his works. 'God,' said the Pharisee in Jesus' parable (praying to himself!), 'I thank you that I am not like other men – robbers, evildoers, adulterers – or even like this tax collector. I fast twice a week and give a tenth of all that I get' (*Luke 18:11–12*).

THE DEVIL'S MARTYRS

Examine any religion that human ingenuity has ever devised and you will discover that it is based ultimately on the idea that man can somehow or other square accounts with God, that his 'good works' will somehow tip the scales in his favour. Paul tells us that it was the cardinal error of the Jews to suppose that they could justify themselves before God by their works. 'I can testify about them,' he says, 'that they are zealous for God, but their zeal is not based on knowledge. Since they did not know the righteousness that comes from God and sought to establish their own, they did not submit to God's righteousness' (*Rom. 10:2–3*). They were what Luther called 'the devil's martyrs', taking endless pains to go to hell. For, as he pointed out, 'We no more earn heaven by good works than babies can earn their food and drink by crying and howling!' George Whitefield agreed wholeheartedly: 'Works? Works? A man get to heaven by works? I would as soon think of climbing to the moon on a rope of sand!'

Those seeking to satisfy God by keeping His law do not realise what obstacles they face. To begin with, they are 'required to obey the whole law' (*Gal. 5:3*). So to fail at one point is to fail completely. Says James, 'For whoever keeps the whole law and yet stumbles at just one point is guilty of breaking all of it' (*Jas. 2:10*). Moreover, failure is attended by a curse, since 'All who rely on observing the law are under a curse, for it is written: "Cursed is everyone who does not continue to do everything written in the Book of the Law"' (*Gal. 3:10*).

Not that that has deterred some intrepid souls! There are those who have felt that they could render a perfect obedience – obedience of the whole man to the whole law for the whole of their lives. Saul of Tarsus, once the typical Pharisee, was of their number. Bounded as his thinking was by externals, he felt that he had succeeded! He was, he claimed, 'faultless' as regards the righteousness of the law (*Phil. 3:6*). But when it finally dawned on him that God sees the hidden motives of the heart, he realised that he had broken the law by coveting.

That sounded the death-knell to all his grandiose schemes of justifying himself before God. It shattered his smugness. He now realised that the whole venture was doomed to failure from the outset. Far from bringing justification, the law had actually uncovered sin and had then proceeded even to incite it. He now knew that 'no-one will be declared righteous in his (God's) sight by observing the law; rather, through the law we become conscious of sin' (*Rom. 3:20*). He began to feel something of 'sin's foul bondage'. He realised for the first time that God's law, which is 'holy, righteous and good', is essentially spiritual, while he was 'unspiritual, sold as a slave to sin' (*Rom. 7:7–14*).

A PURE HEART

It is this spirituality of the law that man under conviction sees so clearly. His good works and outward conformity to imposed standards become an irrelevancy, for it is the state of the heart that matters before God. 'Surely,' cried David in an anguish of conviction, 'you desire truth in the inner parts . . . Create in me a pure heart, O God, and renew a steadfast spirit within me . . . You do not delight in sacrifice, or I would bring it; you do not take pleasure in burnt offerings. The sacrifices of God are a broken spirit: a broken and contrite heart, O God, you will not despise' (*Psa. 51:6,10,16–17*).

This is surely the basic distinction between holiness and man's petty morality. In Charles Hodge's striking comparison, 'The two things differ in nature as much as a clean heart from clean clothes'. When Samuel was tempted to be over-impressed with externals, God rebuked him with the words, 'Man looks at the outward appearance, but the Lord looks at the heart' (*1 Sam. 16:7*).

What is it that the law demands? Absolute perfection! 'Love the Lord your God with all your heart and with all your soul and with all your mind . . . And love your neighbour as yourself' (*Matt. 22:37,39*). That means perfection in every thought, word and deed, every second of our lives from the cradle to the grave. The slightest deviation at any point disqualifies us from God's heaven. So we are all of us doomed to failure before we ever begin. Small wonder that Paul should cry out in abject despair,

'What a wretched man I am! Who will rescue me from this body of death?' (*Rom. 7:24*). And it was the law, so despised by the Antinomians, that brought Paul to that point.

So it all comes down to man's basic problem – sin! And who can remove the burden and guilt of sin? Who can make amends for even one sin, let alone many? Will the relentless life-long effort of the religious zealot make atonement? Let Toplady answer:

> Not the labours of my hands
> Can fulfil Thy law's demands;
> Could my zeal no respite know,
> Could my tears for ever flow,
> All for sin could not atone.

It is to this subject of sin that we now turn our attention.

5: *A Vile Sinner*

The Bible views sin from many different angles. Sometimes it is represented as missing the mark – falling short of the glory of God (*Rom. 3:23*). It may be seen as spiritual adultery. 'You adulterous people,' cries James, 'don't you know that friendship with the world is hatred towards God?' (*Jas. 4:4*). At times sin appears as moral perversion, 'We all, like sheep, have gone astray; each of us has turned to his own way' (*Isa. 53:6*). At other times sin is shown to be the base ingratitude of rebellion against a kind God. 'I reared children and brought them up, but they have rebelled against me' (*Isa. 1:2*).

The Apostle John defines sin as 'lawlessness' (*1 Jn. 3:4*). It has since been described as 'any thought, word or deed contrary to God's law' or (better) as 'lack of conformity to the moral law of God, either in state, disposition or act'. The vital element here is that it is God's law that constitutes the yardstick of judgment – which means that Antinomians are wrong from the start. That makes it essential ιo introduce here a statement on the nature of sin. Wrong views of sin radically affect a man's theology, especially his view of such vital matters as evangelism, repentance and sanctification.

NATURE V. NURTURE

Modern man, if he accepts the idea of sin at all, relates it to nurture, not nature. It is all a question of one's environ-

[38]

ment and upbringing. Give a man a perfect environment and he will himself be perfect. But it was in God's paradise that perfect Adam fell! How much more readily would fallen man fail if he could be returned to paradise!

The Bible takes a much more radical – and realistic – view of sin. On the biblical view, man is already morally twisted when he is born. His whole nature is warped, with an inbuilt bias to sin. 'Surely,' cried David, 'I was sinful at birth, sinful from the time my mother conceived me' (*Psa. 51:5*). That is the confession of one of history's most honest adulterers. He did not blame society, he blamed himself. And Scripture repeatedly corroborates this diagnosis of sin as congenital. 'Even from birth,' says the psalmist, 'the wicked go astray; from the womb they are wayward and speak lies' (*Psa. 58:3*).

God's Word therefore makes it quite clear that sin resides in the heart, the very citadel of man's being. As Jeremiah reminds us, 'The heart is deceitful above all things and beyond cure' (*Jer. 17:9*). Nature, not nurture, is the culprit.

Our Lord had to deal with some early devotees of the nurture theory – the Pharisees. Like their modern counterparts, they could explain human sin and defilement quite easily. In their view, it was due to failure to wash before meals! Our Lord countered their glib diagnosis with one of the most devastating analyses of human defilement ever uttered. 'What comes out of a man is what makes him unclean. For from within, out of men's hearts, come evil thoughts, sexual immorality, theft, murder, adultery, greed, malice, deceit, lewdness, envy, slander, arrogance and folly. All these evils come from inside and make a man unclean' (*Mk. 7:20–23*).

Our Lord thus demonstrates that man, far from being free, is nothing but the bondslave of desires and passions. The psychologist calls them 'drives'. The great Apostle –

before his conversion that paragon of all the virtues! – frankly confesses that 'we too were foolish, disobedient, deceived and enslaved by all kinds of passions and pleasures. We lived in malice and envy, being hateful and hating one another' (*Titus 3:3*).

In an interesting passage in his Epistle to the Ephesians, Paul distinguishes two types of passion – carnal and mental: 'All of us also lived among them at one time, gratifying the cravings of our sinful nature and followed its desires and thoughts' (*Eph. 2:3*).

Anyone with half an eye can recognize those who are the slaves of carnal passions – men and women enslaved to food, drink, drugs, and sex. Less obvious are the passions of the mind – pride, envy, jealousy, malice and a host of other cravings which hold men in thrall. Small wonder that Joseph Alleine should exclaim, 'O miserable man, what a deformed monster has sin made you! God made you "a little lower than the angels"; sin has made you little better than the devils!'[27]

TOTAL DEPRAVITY

Theologians refer to man's condition in sin as 'total depravity'. By this they do not mean that man is totally steeped in sin and debauchery. That would be manifestly untrue. There are 'good pagans' whose lives and 'good works' often put Christians to shame. Total depravity means that sin has affected every faculty of man's being so that nothing he does is done with a single eye to God's glory – which is what God's law requires. Everything is done from a wrong motive – and a wrong motive is the fly in the ointment which infects everything it touches. It is

[27]Alleine, Joseph. *An Alarm to the Unconverted* (1959), p. 21. Banner of Truth.

like a drop of ink in a glass of water which colours it all, though never so slightly.

Such 'good works' as man performs may appear glorious to the onlooker, since he cannot see the heart or the motive behind them. But they are what the Puritans called 'splendid sins', for sins they are. And God who reads us all like an open book dismisses them as 'filthy rags' (*Isa. 64:6*).

Under 'original sin' theologians include what they call 'original guilt' – the guilt attaching to Adam for presuming to break God's law (*Gen. 2:17*). By this one act of disobedience he brought sin and death into the world. And as our representative, he dragged us all down with him (*Rom. 5:12*). Man did, of course, die physically, but the death which sin brought in its train was not primarily physical but spiritual (*Eph. 2:1*). Man forfeited fellowship with God and became a child of the devil (*Jn. 8:44*). Worst of all, man found himself at enmity with the God whose law demands a perfection that man cannot produce. 'The sinful mind', says Paul, 'is hostility to God. It does not submit to God's law, nor can it do so. Those controlled by the sinful nature cannot please God' (*Rom. 8:7–8*).

So God's law is again the focus of attention. 'The sinful mind does not submit to God's law, nor can it do so.' This is man the rebel against God's rule, man the lawbreaker, man the Antinomian. As such, he is under God's judgment, an object of God's holy anger or wrath. 'Let no-one deceive you with empty words', warns the Apostle Paul, 'for because of such things God's wrath comes on those who are disobedient' (*Eph. 5:6*). Man's first need is to be reconciled to God. And this is possible only through Christ's death.

CHRIST THE END OF THE LAW

As we have seen, man is by birth and practice in a hopeless plight. God's law demands total perfection – and that no man can possibly provide. He is therefore under condemnation and as such is excluded from God's heaven. He needs someone who can fulfil the law on his behalf and so provide him with a righteousness that will give him favour with God and entrance to heaven.

And it is God Himself who has provided the remedy. When the first Adam plunged the whole human race into perdition by his sin, God sent a second Adam – or rather, the last Adam – to redeem the situation.

> O loving wisdom of our God!
> When all was sin and shame,
> A second Adam to the fight
> And to the rescue came.
>
> (*J. H. Newman*)

The Apostle Paul puts it in a nutshell: 'Christ is the end of the law so that there may be righteousness for everyone who believes' (*Rom. 10:4*). This does not mean, as the lawless impiously suppose, that Christ has brought our relationship to the law to an end and that we have therefore finished with it. It means that Christ is the perfection of the law. He embodies in His person as the God-man the righteousness which the law requires of man. The law therefore leads to Him as its 'end'.

THE LAW FULFILLED

Christ suffered in His sinless body the punishment for sin demanded by God's law, and that punishment was death. He fulfilled in His sinless life and sacrificial death all the law's demands. As a result, all who believe in Him find Him 'the end of the law for righteousness'. His righteousness is imputed to them, as though it were their own. And that gains them entrance to heaven.

We must consider this in more detail. Christ is 'the end of the law for righteousness' in the sense that He perfectly fulfilled all the requirements of God's moral law down to the minutest detail. He honoured the law by a life of pristine purity. Negatively, He resisted every enticement to evil; positively, He lived a life which reflected at every point the ineffable holiness of God.

When He first came to earth as the Babe of Bethlehem, it was to satisfy the law's demands. 'But when the time had fully come, God sent his Son, born of a woman, born under law, to redeem those under law, that we might receive the full rights of sons' (*Gal. 4:4–5*). It was God who prepared a body for Him and He came in it expressly to do God's will (*Heb. 10:5,9*). He could say with the psalmist, 'I desire to do your will, O my God; your law is within my heart' (*Psa. 40:8*). Again, He testified, 'I always do what pleases him' (*Jn. 8:29*).

Thus it was that His whole life was one of loving obedience to the Ten Commandments, which He summarised as all-consuming love to God and man (*Matt. 22:37–40*). Here was Love Incarnate. Small wonder that the Father should testify publicly, 'This is my Son, whom I love; with him I am well pleased' (*Matt. 3:17*). He thus satisfied, as our representative, all the requirements of the Moral Law.

Christ is also 'the end of the law for righteousness' in the sense that He fulfilled all the 'types and shadows' of the ceremonial law. All the Old Testament rites and ceremonies pointed to Christ and were fulfilled in Him. The tabernacle and the temple with all their ritual washings and purifications were types of Christ. In particular, all the animals sacrificed on altars were types of God's sacrificial Lamb who was sacrificed on the altar of Calvary. The writer of the Epistle to the Hebrews reminds us that the blood of bulls and goats could never take away sins. But Christ's blood could do so – and did!

> Not all the blood of beasts,
> On Jewish altars slain,
> Could give the guilty conscience peace
> Or wash away the stain.
> But Christ, the heavenly Lamb,
> Takes all our sins away;
> A sacrifice of nobler name,
> And richer blood than they.
>
> *(Isaac Watts)*

THE SPOTLESS SACRIFICE

The New Testament, especially the Epistle to the Hebrews, explains at some length how Christ was 'the end of the law for righteousness' when He became the spotless sacrifice demanded as an atonement for sin. John calls Him 'the Lamb of God, who takes away the sin of the world!' (*John 1:29*). Paul asserts that 'Christ, our passover lamb, has been sacrificed' (*1 Cor. 5:7*). This is an explicit reference to Christ as the fulfilment of God's law, which required the death of a lamb in the place of the firstborn. That death typified the propitiation of God's anger against sin. Many such lambs were sacrificed down the running centuries. But not all of them together could deal with the problem of sin. Only Christ could do that, when He came 'to do away with sin by the sacrifice of himself' (*Heb. 9:26*).

> No blood, no altar now:
> The sacrifice is o'er;
> No flame, no smoke, ascends on high,
> The lamb is slain no more.
> But richer blood has flowed from nobler veins,
> To purge the soul from guilt
> And cleanse the reddest stains.
>
> *(Horatius Bonar)*

Christ is also 'the end of the law for righteousness' in the sense that He was the Great High Priest to whom the law pointed. The law required a great high priest who could offer gifts and sacrifices for sins (*Heb. 5:1*). And this, Christ did. The law required a truly human priest who could have compassion on the ignorant and wayward (*Heb. 5:2*). And our Lord was truly Man, 'able to sympathise with our weaknesses . . . and tempted in every way just as we are' (*Heb. 4:15*). The law required a priest who would not die, as did the priests of the Aaronic order (*Heb. 7:23*). And Christ is a priest who 'always lives to intercede' (*Heb. 7:25*). The law required a priest who, unlike the Aaronic priests, was appointed by oath. And the Lord swore an oath to Christ, 'You are a priest for ever, in the order of Melchizedek' (*Heb. 7:17*). The law required a sinless high priest, free from the Aaronic infirmity (*Heb. 7:28*). And Christ was 'holy, blameless, pure, set apart from sinners' (*Heb. 7:26*). The law demanded a better priest than those who had to keep on offering daily sacrifices. And our Lord offered up one sacrifice for sins for ever (*Heb. 7:28; 10:12*).

Christ is thus the Great High Priest envisaged by the law. Having satisfied that law, at every point, He is now at God's right hand in the true tabernacle – that pitched by God, not by man. He is there by virtue of His own blood, not that of bulls and goats. And unlike Aaronic high priests, who entered the earthly holy of holies only once a year, He has entered the heavenly holy of holies once for all. This is the final proof that His sacrifice has been accepted as satisfaction for the violation of God's holy law. It is by that blood that man may now enter into the holiest (*Heb. 10:19*).

> Before the throne of God above
> I have a strong, a perfect plea,
> A great High Priest, whose Name is Love,
> Who ever lives and pleads for me.
>
> (*Charitie L. Smith*)

So Christ is 'the end of the law for righteousness' – not, however, to all mankind, but only 'for everyone who believes'.

6: *Turn or Burn!*

It is the work of the Holy Spirit of God to lead a soul through conviction of sin to conversion, and it is to that subject that we now turn.

It is customary to divide conversion into two elements – repentance and faith. In doing so, we are simply reflecting the Apostle Paul's theology, for he testified to both Jews and Greeks 'that they must turn to God in repentance and have faith toward our Lord Jesus' (*Acts 20:21*).

Antinomians, in their anxiety to exalt free grace, began to disparage repentance as a 'work'. They pointed out (quite rightly) that the Apostle Paul had stated clearly that 'a man is justified by faith apart from observing the law' (*Rom. 3:28*). As man is justified by faith alone, they deduced (quite wrongly) that repentance must be rigidly excluded as a 'good work' coming between the soul and salvation.

SUBVERTING THE GOSPEL

This cordial distaste for preaching repentance has characterised some sections of the Christian church down the running centuries. Among a number of eminent writers we may cite Dr Robert Anderson, who states quite categorically that repentance has no place in gospel preaching.[28] He rests his case on the consideration that

[28]Anderson, Robert. *The Gospel and its Ministry* (1907), p. 58. James Nisbet.

John does not once use the words 'repent' and 'repentance' either in his Gospel or in his epistles, and Paul uses the word 'repentance' in only one chapter of the Epistle to the Romans. But the arguments from Scripture are irresistibly strong and do not depend upon counting words. If we had no other argument – and we have many – it should suffice to say that Christ Himself taught the absolute necessity of repentance. He warned the unbelieving Jews, 'Unless you repent, you too will all perish' (*Luke 13:3*), and told His disciples to preach repentance among all nations.

Nevertheless, the view that one may evangelise without calling on men and women to repent is now widespread among evangelicals. During evangelistic campaigns, I have been told more than once by team leaders that repentance can 'come later'. That may mean years later – years after an enquirer has professed conversion. This is surely to subvert the Christian gospel.

We therefore look now at the biblical view of repentance. We note in the first place that repentance is nothing that man produces. It is the gift of God to both Jews and Gentiles (*Acts 5:31; 11:18*). This means that the glory must be God's alone, for He is the Giver. The recipient has nothing to brag about. As the apostle reminds the Corinthians, 'Who makes you different from anyone else? What do you have that you did not receive? And if you did receive it, why do you boast as though you did not?' (*1 Cor. 4:7*).

Repentance, however, does not take place in a vacuum. God's normal method is to give the call to repentance through preaching. It was Jonah's preaching that caused the Ninevites to repent. And those converted at Pentecost did so as a result of Peter's sermon.

MIND, HEART AND WILL

It cannot be stressed too strongly that repentance is

something which engages man's total personality – mind, heart and will. Any 'gospel' which fails to capture man's total allegiance is therefore by definition not the New Testament gospel. It may indeed be the very snare of Satan – by giving a man a false assurance. A person may stop short at the mind and be content with a theology that leaves his heart and will unmoved. That is sheer intellect-ualism. Others may be stirred emotionally whose minds are unpersuaded by gospel truth and whose lives remain unaffected. But emotionalism is not Christianity. Those whose wills alone are galvanised into action may act from wrong motives, since they have neither understood nor loved God's truth. The blame may lie at the door of the preacher who, in the highly-charged atmosphere of an evangelistic service, has made a direct attack on the will of his hearers by requiring them to 'come forward' or 'stand up and be counted'.

We shall now consider the effect of repentance on mind, heart and will. As we do so, let us bear in mind that these distinctions are made largely for the sake of clarity of thought. The actual process of true repentance is obvi-ously one and indivisible in practice.

CHANGE OF MIND

God's Word makes it quite clear that knowledge of God must come in the first instance to the mind. This highlights the significance of the word 'repent' itself. The Greek word rendered 'repentance' strictly means 'change of mind'. The penitent is one who has a change of mind regarding God's truth.

It is at this point that we see the significance of God's law. For it is God's law that makes the mind aware of sin. Says the Apostle Paul, 'through the law we become conscious of sin' (*Rom. 3:20*). No law, no knowledge of sin; no knowledge of sin, no repentance. How does the law bring knowledge of sin?

It does so in the first place by revealing the truth about God – His glory, His greatness, His holiness and His justice. But also His love, His mercy and His kindness. It may be asked how that brings knowledge of sin. The answer is that, in the light of God's perfect attributes, man is at once made aware of his own corruption.

We see this supremely in the person of Jesus Christ, who was God incarnate. It was a glimpse of Christ's Godlikeness that made Peter exclaim 'Go away from me, Lord, I am a sinful man!' (*Luke 5:8*). Christ is, as J. I. Packer so rightly insists, not only 'grace incarnate' but also 'law incarnate' so that 'meditating on Jesus' words and ways has done more to arouse and deepen a sense of sin than anything else'.[29]

As we have already seen, the law reveals God's standards for mankind – standards incapable of fulfilment. This leaves us helpless and hopeless. But Christ has fulfilled all the requirements of the law on our behalf. In this sense He is 'the end of the law so that there may be righteousness for everyone who believes' (*Rom. 10:4*).

'VILE AND FULL OF SIN'

So a man's mind is first made aware of his sin. Repentance then proceeds to gain the allegiance of the heart, meaning the affections or the emotions. The Latin word 'repent' brings out this emotional element, since it strictly means 'to rue, regret, feel sorry about'. Paul reminds the Corinthians how deeply repentance had affected their hearts. 'Godly sorrow brings repentance that leads to

---

[29]Packer, J. I. *God's Words: Studies of Key Bible Themes* (1981), pp. 8of. Inter-Varsity Press.

salvation and leaves no regret, but worldly sorrow brings death. See what this godly sorrow has produced in you: what earnestness, what eagerness to clear yourselves, what indignation, what alarm, what longing, what concern, what readiness to see justice done' (*2 Cor. 7:10–11*).

The penitent feels himself 'vile and full of sin'. 'I am unworthy,' cried Job. 'I despise myself and repent in dust and ashes' (*Job 40:4; 42:6*). If Job used strong language it was because he felt conviction so keenly. And when a man mourns for sin, he may well cry out, 'What a wretched man I am! Who will rescue me from this body of death?' (*Rom. 7:24*). Like the publican, he may well feel that he cannot even lift his eyes to heaven but beat his breast and say, 'God, have mercy on me, a sinner' (*Luke 18:13*).

ABOUT TURN!

In his burning sense of shame at his sin, the penitent will wish to turn from it all to the One whose holiness has won his heart. It is when the will is engaged that the man turns. Turning lies at the heart of conversion. In the parable of the two sons, the first proved his repentance by actually going to work in the vineyard. It was a one-hundred-and-eighty-degree turn from his original refusal to go (*Matt. 21:28–32*).

The French drill sergeant on the parade ground has something to teach us here. When he wants a radical change of direction, he orders his troops to 'convert'! About turn! And repentance is a radical change of direction in life. It is a turning from a life of sin to a life of holiness. When wicked and unrighteous men repent, they proceed to forsake their old ways as well as their old thoughts (*Isa. 55:7*).

Paul's Thessalonian converts did not merely turn to God from idols, glorious though that was. They turned in order 'to serve the living and true God; and to wait for his Son from heaven' (*1 Thess. 1:9–10*). Paul recalls their radical change of direction. He remembers their 'work produced by faith, and labour produced by love, and endurance produced by hope in our Lord Jesus Christ' (*1 Thess. 1:3–4*). That was the apostle's tangible evidence that their repentance was genuine.

HAND, EYE, MOUTH AND FOOT

The second element in conversion is faith. And when we say 'faith', we do not mean that special gift of faith (*1 Cor. 12:9*) possessed pre-eminently by Christians like George Müller and Hudson Taylor. Nor do we mean that faithfulness which is the fruit of the Spirit (*Gal. 5:22*). We certainly do not mean the 'faith' that people exercise when they board a bus in the belief that it will take them to a given destination. That is 'faith' based on the law of mathematical probability.

We mean 'saving faith' – faith in a Person whom we love, whose word we believe and trust; faith that He will save us from the guilt, the pollution and the power of sin; faith that He will take us to be with Him for ever in heaven.

It is clear that such faith in Christ is not something natural to man, for we are told that 'the man without the Spirit does not accept the things that come from the Spirit of God, for they are foolishness to him, and he cannot understand them, because they are spiritually discerned' (*1 Cor. 2:14*). Indeed, it is worse than that, for man has a fundamental animosity to God. 'The sinful mind is hostile to God. It does not submit to God's law, nor can it do so' (*Rom. 8:7*). All of which means that we need a fundamental change of heart before we can believe, and this happens in the new birth, when God implants the seed of faith.

[52]

Once again, it must be emphasised that faith is not given in a vacuum. It is given as men hear the preached Word. 'Faith', says the apostle, 'comes from hearing the message, and the message is heard through the Word of Christ' (*Rom. 10:17*). James links the rebirth with that word. 'He chose to give us birth through the word of truth, that we might be a kind of firstfruits of all he created' (*Jas. 1:18*).

Before we proceed to a consideration of saving faith itself, we must note its absolute necessity. The unbeliever is under judgment. 'Whoever does not believe stands condemned already because he has not believed in the name of God's one and only Son' (*John 3:18*). Good works cannot save; the law cannot save; only faith can save. We are 'shut up to faith' as the only means of escape from God's wrath. 'The Scripture declares that the whole world is a prisoner of sin, so that what was promised, being given through faith in Jesus Christ, might be given to those who believe' (*Gal. 3:22*).

This caution is necessary in view of the wild assertions of some Antinomians. Tobias Crisp, for example, in a Hyper-Calvinistic fit, assures us that 'an elect person is not in a condemned state while an unbeliever, and should he happen to die before God call him to believe, he would not be lost'.[30] This piece of theological lunacy would cut the nerve of all evangelistic and missionary endeavour. If we may permit ourselves a play on words, it was all due to bias, Crisp.

MIND, HEART AND WILL

Saving faith, like repentance, involves the whole man – mind, heart and will. And truth is presented in the first

---

[30]Crisp, Tobias. *Christ Alone Exalted*. Quoted in *Cyclopaedia of Biblical, Theological and Ecclesiastical Literature*, eds. M'Clintock & Strong (1874), p. 265. Harper.

instance to the mind. There can be no true conversion until the mind gives its assent to the truth. So faith starts in the mind, but it certainly does not stop there – that would be 'believism'.

Faith proceeds to captivate the heart for Christ and His truth. 'I felt I could love Him for ever' becomes the testimony of the soul. We feel we can trust Him and commit ourselves totally to Him.

Finally, faith joins with the will in yielding obedience to the gospel. The New Testament always associates faith with obedience. Paul speaks of 'obedience that comes from faith' (*Rom. 1:5*). And Hebrews 5:9 speaks of Christ as 'the Source of eternal salvation for all who obey him'. In other words, faith acts. And its first act is to forsake all in order to fly to Christ for refuge. Bishop Ryle has expressed it all very graphically:

> 'Saving grace is the *hand* of the soul. The sinner is like a drowning man at the point of sinking. He sees the Lord Jesus Christ holding out help to him. He *grasps* it and is saved. This is faith. (*Heb. 6:18*).
>
> 'Saving faith is the *eye* of the soul. The sinner is like the Israelite bitten by the fiery serpent in the wilderness, and at the point of death. The Lord Jesus Christ is offered to him as the brazen serpent, set up for his cure. He *looks* and is healed. This is faith. (*John 3: 14,15*).
>
> 'Saving faith is the *mouth* of the soul. The sinner is starving for want of food and sick of a sore disease. The Lord Jesus Christ is set before him as the bread of life, and the universal medicine. He *receives* it, and is made well and strong. This is faith. (*John 6:35*).
>
> 'Saving faith is the *foot* of the soul. The sinner is pursued by a deadly enemy, and is in fear of being overtaken. The Lord Jesus Christ is put before him as a strong tower, a hiding place, and a refuge. He *runs* into it and is safe. This is faith. (*Prov. 18:10*).'[31]

[31]Ryle, John Charles. *Old Paths* (1895), pp. 228f. Wm Hunt.

7: Cheap Grace

Scripture is not interested in a mere intellectual assent, in a bare profession of faith, not even in a profession tinged with emotion. It teaches a faith in which the mind is persuaded, the heart warmed and the will bent to obey God's commandments. This is the faith that secures a man's total allegiance for time and for eternity. Paul calls it 'faith expressing itself through love' (*Gal. 5:6*).

This is the whole point of James's passage on faith and works. True faith always works. Indeed, 'faith without deeds is useless' (*Jas. 2:20*). Such a faith is sterile and demonic in nature. James was sure that Abraham was justified by faith – because he demonstrated that faith by his works. So there is no essential conflict between Paul and James. As Fletcher of Madeley put it in answer to the Antinomians, we 'show by St James's works that we have St Paul's faith.' In the words of John Huss, 'Where good works are not without, faith cannot be within.'

EASY BELIEVISM

It is at this point that we face one of the worst features of modern Evangelicalism – easy believism![32] It is something endemic in Antinomianism. It is, in fact, the cardinal error of Sandemanians, whose view on this point is virtually indistinguishable from that of many Anti-

[32]See, e.g., Hulse, Erroll. *The Great Invitation* (1986). Evangelical Press.

nomians. (Robert Sandeman taught that saving faith is
confined to the mind. Faith is simply an intellectual assent
to the facts of the gospel. Feelings (the heart) and
obedience (the will) are rigidly excluded as 'works'. Such
was Sandeman's misguided way of 'safeguarding' justification by faith only).

In all such teaching the main emphasis is put on the
initial confession of Christ with the mouth, based on
Romans 10:9-10: 'If you confess with your mouth, "Jesus
is Lord", and believe in your heart that God raised him
from the dead, you will be saved. For it is with the heart
that you believe and are justified, and it is with your
mouth that you confess and are saved'.

Now it is self-evident that no preacher or evangelist can
possibly read another man's heart. All the emphasis in
handling this verse is therefore put on an individual's
verbal profession. The enquirer 'confesses' with his
mouth that Jesus is Lord; he further professes to believe in
his heart that God has raised Christ from the dead. On this
basis he is confidently pronounced 'saved'.

Despite the obvious fact that the inevitability of
sanctification is clearly here – Jesus as 'Lord' of our lives
–all the emphasis in the Sandemanian viewpoint is placed
on justification, so that Paul is impiously misconstrued as
teaching 'easy believism' – or 'cheap grace', as it has so
rightly been called. You make your confession – prefer-
ably after walking down the aisle – and then you may be
assured you are a Christian and can henceforth be
untroubled by any qualms of conscience. No change of life
need be required – no fruit, no good works, no holiness.
To insist upon these things would be to go back to 'works'.
It would make converts concerned about the subjective
and lead them to forget that all is objective – in Christ.

So such converts are given strict instructions not to
examine themselves (that could be uncomfortable and

disturbing). They are not to seek assurance from signs of holiness in their lives (they might not find any). Feelings are excluded as carnal. They must simply 'look to Jesus'. The advice is sound, but dangerous if offered and taken in isolation from other truths. They say that when doubts arise – as arise they will – they are to be stifled as satanic by believers, who must not be troubled, since they believe in justification 'by faith alone'.

This was the 'bare faith in a bare Christ' of Sandemanianism. It is the intellectual assent called 'faith' which has so often (though, happily, not always) characterised the 'altar call' and the 'public pledge'. But it is not the faith of God's elect.

Dr Kendall lays himself wide open to the charge of advocating cheap grace. He writes, 'I state categorically that the person who is saved – who confesses that Jesus is Lord and believes in his heart that God raised him from the dead – will go to heaven when he dies, no matter what work (or lack of work) may accompany such faith. In other words, no matter what sin (or absence of Christian obedience) may accompany such faith.'[33] Prof Donald Macleod says of this 'misguided' statement, 'To the theologically aware, it immediately suggests Antinomianism. To the general public it is an invitation to live as you please.'[34]

---

[33]Kendall, R. T. *Once Saved, Always Saved* (1983), p. 41. Hodder & Stoughton.

[34]Macleod, Donald in *The Monthly Record of the Free Church of Scotland* (June 1984). Rev. Derek Thomas concurs: '. . . it is a licence to sin that grace may abound' (*Evangelical Presbyterian*, January 1984, pp. 2ff). For further perceptive reviews of *Once Saved, Always Saved*, see Murray, Iain, in *The Banner of Truth* (March 1984, pp. 1ff); Bennett, Christopher, in *Christian Arena* (June 1984, pp. 29f.). Dr William Young had already found evidence in Dr Kendall's D. Phil. thesis of 'the deluded imagination of an Antinomian' (*The Bulwark*, May/June 1980, pp. 15ff.; see also *Gospel Magazine*, Jan/Feb. 1978, pp. 16ff.). Dr Kendall's sermons on Galatians and his *Once Saved, Always Saved* put his Antinomianism beyond all possible

A work published in 1973 goes even further: 'It is possible, even probable, that when a believer out of fellowship falls for certain types of philosophy, if he is a logical thinker, he will become an "unbelieving believer". Yet believers who become agnostics are still saved, they are still born again. You can even become an atheist, but if you once accepted Christ as Saviour, you cannot lose your salvation, even though you deny God' (R. B. Thieme).[35] Maybe Judas Iscariot will be in heaven after all?

This is surely one of the most pressing problems facing the Christian church at the present time. She is producing great numbers of people who have been through some process described as 'conversion' or 'the new birth' but who give no evidence of new life. When a child is born into this world, he will tend to show some sign of life. He may even produce screams calculated to burst every eardrum within earshot. He will certainly breathe! Persistent failure to do so will lead to the melancholy conclusion that the midwife has a stillbirth on her hands.

EASY BELIEVISM RAMPANT

The most glaring example of rampant easy-believism is in the United States of America. Even conservative estimates in that country put the number of those 'born again' at thirty per cent. Some would put it as high as fifty! That would spell revival on a scale totally without precedent in the long history of the Christian church. 'And earth is heaven now' in the USA, you might think. But even a

---

doubt. When six of the twelve deacons at Westminster Chapel charged him with this heresy, they were dismissed. Dr Kendall has published a defence (*Westminster Record*, March 1985, pp. 14ff.). The six orthodox ex-deacons have recorded the relevant facts.

[35]Thieme, R. B. *Apes and Peacocks or the Pursuit of Happiness* (1973), p. 23. Published by the author.

cursory glance would reveal that the 'heaven' is closer to hell. Lawlessness abounds. Social Antinomianism is everywhere evident – even in the churches. There is no evidence that millions 'professing Christ' have actually been 'turned from darkness to light and from the power of Satan to God' (*Acts 26:18*). But when God acts in revival, multitudes of lives are changed and society itself is cleansed as the world is turned upside down.

The Antinomian answer to this dilemma is to assert that there are Christians and Christians. Some, they say, are justified and sanctified. Some are 'merely' justified but they do not opt for sanctification. To this subject we will return later.

8: *His For Ever*

The Scripture makes it crystal-clear that every child of God is eternally secure. Our blessed Lord lent the weight of his infallible authority to this truth when He said, 'My sheep listen to my voice; I know them, and they follow me. I give them eternal life, and they shall never perish, no-one can snatch them out of my hand. My Father, who has given them to me, is greater than all; no-one can snatch them out of my Father's hand' (*John 10:27–29*).

The Apostle Paul taught the same truth with equal certainty: 'He who began a good work in you will carry it on . . . until the day of Christ Jesus' (*Phil. 1:6*). The believer's security is therefore an objective fact, whether he feels it or not. But God desires that every Christian should enjoy assurance – the subjective personal conviction that he is secure in Christ for ever.

It was with this very purpose of bringing assurance to his readers that John wrote his First Epistle. He says so: 'I write these things to you who believe on the name of the Son of God so that you may know that you have eternal life' (*1 John 5:13*). This introduces us to the first of three ways by which we may know we have eternal life – the Word of God itself.

The believer is encouraged to take the clear statements of God's Word and apply them to himself. He may, for instance, take the statement of Christ in John 3:36, 'Whoever believes in the Son has eternal life'. Using a process of reasoning known as a syllogism, he argues something like this. 'Christ said that whoever believes in the Son has eternal life. I believe in the Son. Therefore I have eternal life'. Many have found true assurance in this way.

THE TESTS OF LIFE

There is, however, a second method of arriving at assurance. This is by applying what are often termed 'the tests of life' – tests by which we may determine whether or not we are Christians. Those who pass the tests may be assured that they have eternal life. What are these tests? We can find some of them in John's First Epistle.

The first test is doctrinal. Says John, 'Everyone who believes that Jesus is the Christ is born of God' (*1 John 5:1*). So those born of God believe in Christ's Deity – His Godhead. John does not mean simply His Divinity – even Jehovah's Witnesses believe in that. It is not enough to believe that Jesus is the Son of God – unless by that we mean that He is God the Son. Christians are those who can say with Thomas, 'My Lord and my God!'

Secondly, have I been given the Spirit of God? 'And this,' says John, 'is how we know that he lives in us: We know it by the Spirit he gave us' (*1 John 3:24*). To use Pauline language, that Spirit is the Holy Spirit of promise who seals believers and is the deposit guaranteeing their inheritance (*Eph. 1:13–14*). So to have the Spirit is certainly to have eternal life.

Thirdly, if I am a Christian, I keep God's commandments, and find them my delight. The apostle writes, 'This is how we know that we love the children of God: by loving God and carrying out his commands. This is love for God: to obey his commands. And his commands are not burdensome' (*1 John 5:2–3*).

It is interesting, though sad, to notice how theological

extremes fail the test at this point, though they do so for different reasons. Legalists seek to keep God's commandments, but life for them is so burdensome that they find no delight in obedience. Small wonder! It is an intolerable burden trying to earn one's salvation by good works! Antinomians, on the other hand, assure us that they enjoy great liberty and delight, but it is not delight in God's commandments, for they do not trouble to keep them. They need to take a leaf out of the book of the psalmist who testified, 'Direct me in the path of your commands, for there I find delight' (*Psa. 119:35*).

Am I conscious of a spiritual conflict in the soul? This is a further indication of regeneration. The Apostle Paul says, 'The sinful nature desires what is contrary to the Spirit, and the Spirit what is contrary to the sinful nature' (*Gal. 5:17*). He means that the soul is a battleground where the Holy Spirit wages a warfare against Satan and his hordes. Those who are aware of this warfare may deduce from that fact that they have eternal life.

We may also test our profession of faith by our attitude to Christian brethren. Do we love them? John says, 'We know that we have passed from death to life, because we love our brothers' (*1 John 3:14*). The apostle does not say that we necessarily like our brothers. A liking is something biological over which we have no control. It would therefore be absurd to require anyone to like something he constitutionally disliked. But we are required to love, for love is the gift of God's grace and a fruit of the Spirit.

We are not, however, to think of love in terms of pure emotion. John proceeds to show what Scripture means by love. Love in the Bible is a practical grace, something that works. God's Son did not just love us in abstraction in heaven. Though equal with God, He took human flesh, 'humbled himself and became obedient to death – even death on a cross!' (*Phil. 2:5–8*). 'And we ought to lay down our lives for our brothers', adds John, the Apostle of Love (*1 John 3:16*). Love is the test.

If a Christian is one who loves the brethren, he is at the same time one who hates sin. He hates it partly because it robs him of blessing and makes his life miserable. But he goes well beyond such a subjective reason for hating sin. He hates it because it took his Lord to the accursed Tree. And he hates it because it robs God of the glory which is His rightful due. It is this which makes him cry out with William Cowper,

> I hate the sins that made Thee mourn
> And drove Thee from my breast.

So if I hate sin, I am entitled to conclude that I am a child of God, for no unbeliever ever yet hated sin.

Show me someone who hates sin and I will show you someone who loves holiness. It must follow as the night the day. John says that the sons of God will one day be like Christ. On that day they will see Him as He is. 'Everyone who has this hope in him purifies himself, just as he is pure' (*1 John 3:2–3*). Loving holiness is the test.

The Apostle John, in common with all the other New Testament writers, makes it abundantly clear that there are only two classes of people in this world. One is either in the light or in the darkness; one either loves the brethren or one hates them; one is either holy or unholy. Dr Martyn Lloyd-Jones puts this teaching in his trenchant manner, so reminiscent of the Apostle John. 'If you are not holy,' he avers, 'you are not a Christian'. He then fires a Johannine broadside against the hypocrite: 'If you claim to love Christ and yet are living an unholy life, there is only one thing to be said about you: you are a bare-faced liar!'[36] In John's words: 'The man who says, "I know him," but

---

[36]Lloyd-Jones, D. M. *Darkness and Light* (1982), p. 345. Banner of Truth.

does not do what he commands is a liar, and the truth is not in him' (*1 John 2:4*). Let every man examine himself.

As a final test of life, we may add the desire to know God. It is a desire for a personal knowledge of God Himself, not merely for the blessings that He can give.

> My goal is God Himself,
> Not joy, nor peace, nor even blessings,
> But Himself, my God.
> His, His to lead me there, not mine but His,
> At any cost, dear Lord, by any road.

Such was the heart-felt desire of the psalmist. 'As the deer pants for streams of water, so my soul pants for you, O God. My soul thirsts for God, for the living God. When can I go and meet with God?' (*Psa. 42:1–2*). To know God in Christ was the Apostle Paul's burning desire. Indeed, it was his one ambition in life. His testimony was, 'I consider everything a loss compared to the surpassing greatness of knowing Christ Jesus my Lord, for whose sake I have lost all things. I consider them rubbish, that I may gain Christ and be found in him . . . I want to know Christ' (*Phil. 3:8–10*).

A person who senses in his soul even the faintest glimmerings of such a desire for God need not doubt for a moment that he is an heir of eternal life.

ABBA, FATHER

There is, however, an even higher form of assurance, and that is the witness of the Holy Spirit Himself. This is something well beyond the logical syllogism or even the tests of life. It is a direct and infallible assurance that God is my Father and I am His son in an everlasting relationship that no power in heaven or earth or hell can sever. Paul speaks of it in the words: 'those who are led by the Spirit of God are sons of God. For you did not receive a spirit that makes you a slave again to fear, but you received the Spirit of sonship. And by him we cry, "*Abba*, Father." The Spirit himself testifies with our spirit that we are God's children. Now if we are children, then we are heirs – heirs of God and co-heirs with Christ' (*Rom. 8:14–17*).

It was a deep yearning for this highest type of assurance that constrained the poet to write:

> Tell me Thou art mine, O Saviour,
> Grant me an assurance clear;
> Banish all my dark misgivings,
> Still my doubting, calm my fear.
> O, my soul within me yearneth
> Now to hear Thy voice divine;
> So shall grief be gone for ever,
> And despair no more be mine.

And when that assurance is given, we may boldly sing:

> From Him who loves me now so well
> What power my soul can sever?
> Shall life or death, shall earth or hell?
> No! I am His for ever.

(James G. Small)

9: *The Christian Life*

Peter believed in justification by faith alone as strongly as any of the other apostles. But along with them he also believed that assurance of salvation turns in measure on the extent to which Christians add to that faith. They need to furnish it out with other graces, so that it becomes full-orbed. Says Peter, 'For this very reason, make every effort to add to your faith goodness; and to goodness knowledge; and to knowledge self-control; and to self-control perseverance; and to perseverance godliness; and to godliness brotherly kindness; and to brotherly kindness love' (*2 Peter 1:5–7*). He adds that this is the way to make our calling and election sure. It is the high road to assurance.

This is partly why Paul presses on Christians the duty of examining themselves. 'Examine yourselves', he tells the Corinthians, 'to see whether you are in the faith; test yourselves. Do you not realise that Christ Jesus is in you – unless, of course, you fail the test?' (*2 Cor. 13:5*). Paul knew that if one of the Twelve could prove to be a devil, there might well be others like him among the professing Christians in Corinth.

If some Antinomians had defended Paul, others now attacked him. Said one, 'If Christ be my sanctification, what need have I to look to any thing in myself to evidence my justification?'[37] Others argued: 'Self-examination may

---

[37]Quoted in Kevan, Ernest F. *The Grace of Law* (1964). p. 219. Carey Kingsgate.

be dangerous, maybe I will deceive myself. So it is better for me to rely solely on the immediate witness of the Spirit.'

The simple answer to all that is that God requires us to examine ourselves. That is sufficient in itself, quite apart from the consideration that Church history witnesses to the tragic possibility of listening to seducing spirits, who persuade men that they are Christ's when in fact they are Satan's dupes. 'Belief in the inner light', said J. S. Whale, 'may be the shortest road to the outer darkness'.

TWELVE SEARCHING QUESTIONS

Unpopular though it may be, if we are serious about holiness, we shall need to spend time examining ourselves – the very thing the Antinomian discourages. We are not called to a life of introspection – that is morbid and unhealthy. But we are called to 'examine' ourselves (*2 Cor. 13:5*). This exhortation may sound novel to modern ears. At one time, however, it was observed scrupulously by the godly. Fletcher of Madeley suggested to his people the following questions for self-examination:

1. Did I awake spiritual, and was I watchful in keeping my mind from wandering this morning when I was rising?
2. Have I this day got nearer to God in times of prayer, or have I given way to a lazy, idle spirit?
3. Has my faith been weakened by unwatchfulness, or quickened by diligence this day?
4. Have I this day walked by faith and eyed God in all things?
5. Have I denied myself in all unkind words and thoughts; have I delighted in seeing others preferred before me?
6. Have I made the most of my precious time, as far as I had light, strength and opportunity?

7. Have I kept the issues of my heart in the means of grace, so as to profit by them?
8. What have I done this day for the souls and bodies of God's dear saints?
9. Have I laid out anything to please myself when I might have saved the money for the cause of God?
10. Have I governed well my tongue this day, remembering that in a multitude of words there wanteth not sin?
11. In how many instances have I denied myself this day?
12. Do my life and conversation adorn the gospel of Jesus Christ?

Let every man examine himself.

HOLINESS AND GROWTH

Bible scholars tend to consider the subject of sanctification under two heads. One is often termed 'positional' or 'definitive' sanctification, the other 'ethical' or 'practical' sanctification. The first we shall consider much more briefly than the second, to which vastly more space is given in Holy Scripture.

Positional sanctification is applied scripturally to things as well as people. It means that certain things or people are set apart (separated) from secular use to God and His purpose. In this sense it is applied, for example, to Mount Sinai and to the Mount of Transfiguration, which Peter calls 'sacred' (*2 Pet. 1:18*). It is likewise applied to the tabernacle and the temple, which were reserved exclusively for divine worship. As the vessels of both tabernacle and temple were also reserved exclusively for religious purposes, they are described in Scripture as 'holy' (*Exod. 40:10ff*). The seventh day was 'sanctified' in this sense (*Gen. 2:3*).

This usage of the word is applied to the Old Testament prophets (*Lk. 1:70*). The New Testament apostles and prophets are likewise separated to God (*Eph. 3:5*). It is thus used of Christ Himself. We read that the Father set Him apart and He sanctified Himself (*Jn. 10:36; 17:19*). As Christ is the Holy One from all eternity, this cannot possibly have a moral reference and therefore means that Christ the God-Man was set apart for the particular purpose of redeeming fallen mankind.

It is in this sense that Christians can be said to be sanctified before they are justified (*1 Cor. 6:11; 1 Pet. 1:2*). Christ thus set His people aside for Himself when He died on the cross. Says the writer of the Epistle to the Hebrews, 'Jesus also, that he might sanctify the people with his own blood, suffered without the gate' (*Heb. 13:12*).

Another meaning of 'sanctify' is 'to make holy in practice and experience'. The theologically minded will love the definition given by Berkhof: 'Sanctification is that gracious and continuous operation of the Holy Spirit by which He delivers the justified sinner from the pollution of sin, renews his whole nature in the image of God, and enables him to perform good works.'[38]

The God who chose His people before time began and called them to Christ by His grace will one day take them to glory. But before He glorifies them, He will sanctify them. He has told us that sanctification is His will for us (*1 Thess. 4:3*). He is Himself holy and He intends to make us holy too.

A PROCESS

Unlike justification, sanctification is a process. It begins with the new birth and will be perfected only in the glory everlasting. The Apostle Peter inculcates this principle of

[38]Berkhof, L. *Systematic Theology* (1958), p. 532. Banner of Truth.

growth when he addresses the 'baby' readers of his First Epistle. 'Like newborn babies,' he says, 'crave pure spiritual milk, so that by it you may grow' (*1 Pet. 2:2*). He is emphasising that sanctification begins with regeneration (the new birth) and is something progressive. The Apostle John in turn emphasises this progressive element. If Peter writes to 'newborn babies', John writes to 'children', 'young men' and 'fathers' (*1 Jn. 2:12–14*). In similar vein, the writer to the Hebrews distinguishes between the 'infants', who are still on milk, and the 'mature', who have progressed to solids (*Heb. 5: 12–14*). See 1 Corinthians 3: 1–2 to the same effect.

It must again be said that some Antinomians flatly deny this whole biblical concept of growth. On their view (which again confuses justification with sanctification), a Christian is totally sanctified at conversion and so he is neither more nor less holy from that moment to the moment of his death.[39] This opinion is no mere seventeenth-century error. It again became popular in the seventies of the last century, since when it has been widely taught in somewhat modified form. This approach sees the Christian life in terms of 'counteraction'. On this view, holiness is something outside the Christian, whose essential personality remains unchanged. It has often been compared to a lifebelt, which holds a Christian up in a sea of troubles and without which he would sink. But again it is a virtual denial of regeneration and growth, since the man himself remains unchanged.

RECIPE FOR GROWTH

How, then, does the Christian grow? Many answers could be given to that question. One of them we have already

---

[39]Stated and refuted in *Wesley's Works* (1877), vol. X, pp. 275f. Wesleyan-Methodist Book-Room.

mentioned – by studying God's Word! This is milk for the babe and solid food for the weaned. No-one can grow who does not feed regularly on the Bible. Here is everything we could ever need. Says Paul, 'All scripture is God-breathed and is useful for teaching, rebuking, correcting and training in righteousness, so that the man of God may be thoroughly equipped for every good work' (*2 Tim. 3:16–17*). Paul is referring to God's law. Says Calvin, commenting on this passage, 'The law by teaching, warning, admonishing and correcting, prepares us for every good work.'

We may illustrate the 'profitability' of which Paul speaks by reference to Psalm 119, that storehouse of treasures on the Law of God. Here are just a few principles extracted from the psalm – there are many more. This is the psalmist's recipe for growth in grace.

He prays God to open his eyes to see the wonderful things in God's law (*18*), in which he takes great delight (*47*), and which he is prepared to obey diligently (*4*). He hides God's Word in his heart as a shield from sin (*11*), as he meditates on it all day long (*97*). He seeks God with all his heart (*10*) in prayer (*17*) and praise (*164*) and a concern for God's cause (*136*). He longs to be free from sin (*133*), which he hates (*163*). So he accepts chastisement gladly (*75*). Strengthened by fellowship with God's people (*63*), he gives a bold witness to the world (*46*). Hallelujah! We must surely agree with Matthew Henry, 'When the law of God is written in our hearts, our duty will be our delight'.

THE GOOD FIGHT

While speaking clearly of our duty, the Bible still asserts that sanctification is fundamentally the work of the Holy Spirit. 'You were sanctified,' says Paul, 'by the Spirit of our God' (*1 Cor. 6:11*). So he speaks of 'the sanctifying work of the Spirit' (*2 Thess. 2:13*).

The fact that God's Spirit is the prime agent in sanctification has led some Christians into the dangerous error of passivity. If God does everything, they need do nothing – or so they argue. This kind of reasoning is evident in the illustration of the lifebelt, which clearly suggests that the Christian is totally passive. C. H. A. Trumbull is 'credited' (if that is the right word) with coining the expression 'Let go and let God'. In response to the Christian's surrender, God takes over and does everything. This has become a popular formula in some circles, where it is thought to epitomise the biblical view of sanctification. But it is in fact a delusion. One may discover that to let go is to let Satan.

THE PARADOX

The biblical answer to the problem lies in the paradox that while God works in us, we must also work. While it is true to say that we are God's workmanship, it is also true that we are called upon to make every effort. While the strength is God's, the resultant effort is ours. 'Sanctification is all the work of God and all the work of man' ('Rabbi' Duncan). So John Monsell was right when he wrote:

> Fight the good fight with all thy might;
> Christ is thy strength, and Christ thy right.

The Apostle Paul, as usual, had already stated the paradox perfectly: 'Work out your salvation with fear and trembling, for it is God who works in you to will and to act according to his good pleasure' (*Phil. 2:12–13*). It is God who prompts the desire in our hearts to please Him, and then supplies the power to do His will.

A HOLY WAR

It seems quite incredible that anyone could read the New Testament without noticing the repeated calls to action. The Christian cannot afford to sit by passively. As J. C. Ryle says, 'There is no holiness without a warfare.'[40] The Christian is called to a holy war against the world, the flesh and the devil that once enslaved him. He is under orders to 'fight the good fight of the faith' (*1 Tim. 6:12*). It is a fight against satanic hordes in which he will need to put on 'the full armour of God' (*Eph. 6:10–20*).

> Stand, then, in His great might,
> With all His strength endued;
> But take, to arm you for the fight,
> The panoply of God.
> To keep your armour bright
> Attend with constant care,
> Still serving in your Captain's sight,
> And watching unto prayer.
>
> (*Charles Wesley*)

The Christian life is also compared to a race for a crown. The Christian will therefore need to discard every hindrance and every besetting sin so that he can run unhindered (*1 Cor. 9:24–27; Heb. 12:1–2*).

> Awake, my soul, stretch every nerve,
> And press with vigour on;
> A heavenly race demands thy zeal
> And an immortal crown.
>
> (*Philip Doddridge*)

No-one has ever won a fight or a race by merely sitting back and waiting for things to happen.

This is no mere academic matter. We are not writing of

[40]Ryle, J. C. *Holiness* (1952), p. 55. James Clarke.

those whose lives are spent idling luxuriously in some ivory tower. We are concerned with men and women facing the hard realities of life in a hostile world. To tell such people that all they need do is 'let go and let God' is nothing short of criminal. It is a recipe for those 'leaden-eyed despairs' of which the poet Keats writes.

Much could be written on the evil effects of teaching passivity or quietism. Church history bears melancholy witness to the fact that many have made shipwreck of the faith in this heretical sea.

HAPPINESS OR HOLINESS?

One thinks of writers like Hannah Pearsall-Smith, whose *Christian's Secret of a Happy Life* was once a best-seller. This unhappy volume – which has led many to the brink of despair – poses the question, What must the Christian do in his quest for victory? The answer lies in one word – nothing! For sheer distortion of Scripture, Mrs Pearsall-Smith's teaching surely takes some beating. Incidentally, it is known that she died in great misery.

The very title of the Pearsall-Smith book in itself betrays a fundamental misconception. God calls us, not to happiness, but to holiness. Of course, to be holy is of necessity also to be happy, but we are to seek after holiness. 'Sow holiness,' comments George Swinnock, 'and reap happiness'. But, as has often been pointed out, if we seek happiness we shall get neither that nor holiness.

This is all so typical of the man-centred and subjective age in which we live. We are all self-centred by nature and it even infects our Christianity. We are not excited by sermons on the glory of God or the call to holy living. But we will flock in great numbers to hear about 'Victory for me', 'How to succeed in my life' and a host of other addresses offering popular psychology in the guise of Christianity.

God alone knows the heart, and it is not for us to sit in final judgment on others. But we would do well to heed the words of the Apostle Peter, who speaks of the unlearned and unstable who wrest the Scriptures to their own destruction. He ends his second Epistle with the exhortation: 'Therefore, dear friends, since you already know this, be on your guard so that you may not be carried away by the error of lawless men and fall from your secure position. But grow in the grace and knowledge of our Lord and Saviour Jesus Christ. To him be glory both now and for ever! Amen.'

10: 'A Sair Fecht'

A young Christian, flushed with excitement on his return from a convention on victorious living, was putting his pastor right on the true method of sanctification. It was, he insisted, all quite simple. If only Christians would stop struggling against sin and temptation, and hand everything over to the Risen Lord, He would take over and win the victory for them. They had but to lie passive, like clay in the potter's hands. Dr Alexander Whyte, the dour old Scots minister, shook his head sadly, before giving his sobering reply, 'Och, laddie, it's a sair fecht tae the end!' It is the reply found everywhere in the New Testament.

It is 'a sore fight to the end' because of the enemies which the Christian faces – the world, the flesh and the devil – enemies which never cease from attacking us till we breathe our last. We must now turn our attention to the Christian's fight with the flesh – that principle of sin which remains in every saint till the hour of death. What must the Christian do about this principle of sin, sometimes called the old nature?

SINLESS?

The first answer is that the Christian must recognise that he still has the old nature within. Some Antinomians and others have gone astray because they refused to recognise the enemy within. Tobias Crisp – whose heart was, we trust, better than his head – has misled many into believing that Christians are sinless, like their Lord. 'Christ's righteousness,' says Crisp, 'is so imputed to the elect, that they, ceasing to be sinners, are as righteous as He was, and all that he was. Any conviction of sin must therefore be satanic in origin. The feelings of conscience, which tell them that sin is theirs, arise from a want of knowing the truth. It is but the voice of a lying spirit in the hearts of believers that saith they have yet sin wasting their consciences, and lying as a burden too heavy for them to bear.'[41]

John roundly denounces that view as self-deception. 'If we claim to be without sin, we deceive ourselves, and the truth is not in us' (*1 John 1:8*). Sinless perfection is everywhere stated in Scripture to lie in the future. It is only when we see Christ that we shall be perfectly like Him (*1 John 3:2*). The claim to be sinlessly perfect here on earth is described by J. I. Packer as 'the apotheosis of self-deception'. Spurgeon put it more personally: 'I met only one perfect man – and he was a perfect nuisance!'

Others concede that Christians do sin, but it is unnecessary or even blasphemous to confess sin, because God either cannot see their sin or turns a blind eye to it. He certainly would not chastise Christians for it. Such teaching stands self-condemned. It arises from the perennial Antinomian confusion between justification and sanctification. The God who declares us righteous in Christ by imputation will make us holy by imparting that righteousness. Far from ignoring sin in the saints, He abominates it. He intends to make us partakers of His holiness, and chastisement is an essential part of that process. No chastisement, no heaven (*Heb. 12:5ff*).

The second answer is that the Christian must deal radically with his old nature. The New Testament tells him to put it to death – which is what the Authorised

[41]Crisp, Tobias. *Op.cit.*, p. 265.

Version means by 'mortify'. It is to this subject that we now turn our attention.

BE KILLING SIN

The Scripture tells Christians that 'if by the Spirit you put to death the misdeeds of the body, you will live' (*Rom. 8:13*). The Greek here is better rendered 'if you keep on putting to death', suggesting the continuing process. As long as we are in the body we must go on mortifying sin. The Apostle Paul, as usual, adduces his reasons for this.

He tells the Roman Christians that they are no longer carnally minded, but spiritually minded; no longer in the flesh, but in the Spirit. The carnal (i.e. unbelievers) suffer 'death' both in this world and in the next. The spiritual (i.e. Christians) enjoy 'life' both here and in the hereafter. He therefore argues that anything of the flesh that remains in the Christian must be ruthlessly put to death in the Spirit's power. In John Owen's forceful words, 'Be killing sin, or sin will be killing you!'[42]

Paul also tells the Colossians to kill sin. It is the logical thing for Christians to do, since they are dead to the old life and alive in Christ, whose glory they will one day share. From these truths the Apostle concludes, 'Put to death, therefore, whatever belongs to your earthly nature: sexual immorality, impurity, lust, evil desires and greed, which is idolatry . . . rid yourselves of anger, rage, malice, slander and filthy language from your lips. Do not lie to each other' (*Col. 3:5ff*). So the question at once arises, How does one mortify sin?

A WORLD OF INIQUITY

One must first recognise the enormity of the problem that

---

[42] *The Works of John Owen* (1967), vol. VI, p. 9. Banner of Truth.

one faces – that sin is 'a positive and destructive principle endemic in man' (A. M. Hunter). If we follow the Antinomians in their slight views of sin, we shall not take mortification very seriously. But sin is a world of iniquity, a spiritual malignancy at the very heart of the personality.

One must add to this fact the horrifying consideration that sin in the unregenerate becomes progressively worse and more virulent as life proceeds. 'Sin,' says William Gurnall, 'is an hereditary disease that increaseth with age. A young sinner will be an old devil'.[43] That is the simple, unvarnished truth, as any true observer of human life will testify. The hardened criminal with a seared conscience was once a tender-hearted toddler, sensitive to wrong-doing and sin.

One may add to this the melancholy fact that, as John Owen puts it, 'Sin aims always at the utmost . . . Every unclean thought or glance would be adultery if it could . . . every thought of unbelief would be atheism'.[44] What a world of evil an outwardly moral life can conceal!

All of this argues the need for positive action. Mortification is a warfare which must be pursued with diligence. Nor is there any let-up in the conflict while we remain in the body. Says Owen, 'Sin will not otherwise die, but by being gradually and constantly weakened; spare it and it heals its wounds and recovers strength. We must continually watch against the operations of this principle of sin: in our duties, in our calling, in conversation, in retirement, in our straits, in our enjoyments, and in all that we do. If we are negligent on any occasion, we shall suffer by it; every mistake, every neglect is perilous.' This appeal is, of course, addressed only to the believer – one who has already entered into peace with God. No unbeliever can

[43]Gurnall, William. *The Christian in Complete Armour* (1964). Banner of Truth.
[44]*Op.cit.*, p. 12.

obtain peace with God by mortification of sin – or, indeed, by any other activity. That would be justification by works.

NIP SIN IN THE BUD!

We should note at this point the crucial importance of dealing with sin in its initial stages before it can develop. Wisdom dictates that we nip it in the bud. It always seeks to conquer mind, heart and will in the progressive manner outlined by Thomas Aquinas: 'Sin is first a simple suggestion, then a strong imagination, then delight, then assent.'

This is the history of the Fall. Eve first saw the fruit, then lusted for it, and finally took it. James personifies evil and names three generations in the family tree. Evil desire, he says, gives birth to sin, then sin produces death (*Jas. 1: 13–15*). The wise man murders evil desire before it can produce any offspring!

It is surely significant that Scripture lays especial emphasis on mortification of the tongue. The tongue may be small, says James, but it is a hell-kindled fire, a world of iniquity, a restless evil full of deadly poison (*Jas. 3*).

The ancients thought that God has given us two ears but only one tongue so that we might listen more than we speak. He has set two barriers before the tongue – the teeth and the lips – but it breaks through them both!

The psalmist shows us the highway to blessing in this area. It is the way of mortification. He writes, 'Whoever of you loves life and desires to see many good days . . .' What should he do? The modern Christian tends to answer, 'Trust the Lord and pray about it.' But the psalmist has a somewhat different piece of advice to offer:

'Keep your tongue from evil and your lips from speaking lies!' (*Psa. 34:12–13*). We need to deny utterance to words that are untrue or unkind or unnecessary – the sly innuendo, the barbed witticism at another's expense.

11: *Heaven and Our Sins Too?*

Some modern Antinomians assure us that there are two types of Christians. Those in the first category automatically acknowledge the claims of Christ the Lord and proceed to live holy lives in a grand desire to be like Him, to magnify His grace and to show forth His praise. Those in the second category treat sanctification as optional – and promptly opt for sin. Indeed, as one preacher assured me, they may get away with it in this world – without chastisement. They will, however, suffer what he called 'terminal chastisement' at the judgment Seat of Christ and yet be finally saved.[45]

The immediate answer to such an impious suggestion is the biblical assertion that every Christian is subject to chastisement in this world. It is inevitable. It is also an infallible sign of sonship. The writer of the Letter to the Hebrews puts if very bluntly: 'If you are not disciplined (and everyone undergoes discipline), then you are illegitimate children and not true sons' (*Heb. 12:8*). Illegitimate children! He goes on to argue that chastisement is part of the whole process of sanctification, without which nobody can see the Lord. (Read the whole of Hebrews chapter 12.)

DIVIDING CHRIST

We must add that to teach that Christians can opt out of

[45]Kendall, R. T. *Once Saved, Always Saved* (1983), p. 110. Hodder & Stoughton.

holiness is to repeat the error of the Corinthians who divided Christ. This error encourages Christians to believe that they can receive Christ as Saviour only. They may then later deign (if so disposed) to receive Him as Lord.[46] But this is a spiritual and theological monstrosity. Christ *is* Lord, and to receive Him at all is to receive Him as Lord and Saviour. That is indeed His title – 'our Lord and Saviour Jesus Christ'. So Paul describes Christians as those who have 'received Christ Jesus as Lord' (*Col. 2:6*).

Put in other words, this is today's familiar Antinomian error of separating justification from sanctification. And Paul says that it cannot be done. As he reminds the Corinthians, if one is in Christ at all, one receives in Him 'wisdom, righteousness (justification), holiness and redemption' (*1 Cor. 1:30*). The process of salvation is one and indivisible. We cannot pick and choose. It is all or nothing.

AN OPTIONAL EXTRA?

Another way in which the biblical requirement of holiness is still being side-stepped is to interpret belonging to 'the kingdom of God' as an optional extra for *some* Christians – an additional perquisite reserved for those who take holiness seriously. The 'carnal Christian' is said to be outside 'the kingdom'. He will get to heaven all right, but 'as one escaping through the flames' and therefore without reward. His salvation is secure, it is just that he will miss out on any rewards that may be going.[47]

---

[46]See, e.g., Tozer, A. W. *I call it Heresy!* (1974), pp. 9ff. Christian Publications; Lloyd-Jones, D. Martyn, *Christ our Sanctification* (1948), pp. 7ff. Inter-Varsity Fellowship; Chrisope, T. Alan *Jesus is Lord* (1982). Evangelical Press.

[47]Kendall, R. T. *Op.cit.*, pp. 107ff.

This is a serious denial of at least two New Testament passages – one in First Corinthians and the other in Ephesians. 'Do you not know,' says the Apostle, 'that the wicked will not inherit the kingdom of God? Do not be deceived: Neither the sexually immoral nor idolaters nor adulterers nor male prostitutes nor homosexual offenders nor thieves nor the greedy nor drunkards nor slanderers nor swindlers will inherit the kingdom of God' (*1 Cor. 6:9–10*). 'So these carnal Christians will lose out on rewards,' says the Antinomian. 'Rewards?' the apostle rejoins. 'These people are not even Christians!' Listen to Paul as he adds, 'And that is what some of you were. But you were washed, you were sanctified, you were justified in the name of the Lord Jesus Christ and by the Spirit of our God.' That clinches it. No holiness, no heaven! It is the express teaching of our Lord that to be born again and to 'enter the kingdom of God' are inseparable (*John 3:5*).

They may not all realise it, but modern espousers of the view that not all Christians will inherit the kingdom of God are simply repeating an error propounded by Agricola, the Father of modern Antinomianism. Happily for us, Luther was at hand to answer Agricola's 'blasphemous impiety'.

'NO PART IN CHRIST'

Luther traced this error to failure to preach the law – not merely to the sinner (to convict him of his sin and need of Christ), but also to the saint (to teach the absolute necessity of 'crucifying the sinful nature with its passions and desires'). Take away the law, said Luther, and men in their ignorance will live carelessly, comfortable in their sin. Luther then pinpoints one great weakness in Antinomian theology – the failure to teach regeneration, and the holiness which inevitably accompanies it. Writing of the Antinomians, he says:

'These men pretend to preach finely about grace and the remission of sins, but they avoid the doctrine of sanctification and newness of life in Christ – so that men may not be rendered uneasy, but may enjoy uninterrupted consolation. For, whereas they ought to say, "If you are an adulterer, a fornicator, a drunkard, proud, covetous, a usurer, you cannot be a Christian," they say, "Though you are such, only believe in Christ, and you will have no need to fear the law; Christ has fulfilled it all!" They do not see how sanctification follows upon justification, so that a Christian must necessarily be a partaker of the Holy Spirit, and lead a new life: and, if he does not do that, let him know that he has no part in Christ.'[48]

If you think Luther is blunt, the Apostle Paul is more so. He warns us lest any should deceive us with 'vain words' for it is certain that the unholy are those upon whom the wrath of God is coming (*Eph. 5:6*).

THE GOLDEN CHAIN OF REDEMPTION

Current Antinomianism has thought up yet another device to justify the proposition that sanctification is optional. It has reference to what has been termed 'the golden chain of redemption', notably in Romans 8:29. Here the Apostle writes, 'For those God foreknew he also predestinated to be conformed to the likeness of his Son, that he might be the firstborn among many brothers. And those he predestinated, he also called; and those he called, he also justified; and those he justified, he also glorified.' Here we have listed some of the links in the chain of redemption – foreknowledge, predestination, calling,

---

[48]Luther, Martin. Quoted in Scott, John. *The History of the Church of Christ* (1826), p. 329. Seeley & Burnside.

justification and glorification. It has been deduced from this that sanctification must be optional, otherwise the Apostle would have included it in his list.[49] But this is a totally inadmissible deduction. The Apostle is simply demonstrating the inevitability of our being completely and finally redeemed. This is so certain in the eternal purpose of God that Paul describes Christians as already glorified!

Again, this novel theory receives its *coup de grâce* in the passage already quoted from Paul's First Epistle to the Corinthians, where the apostle writes, 'It is because of him that you are in Christ Jesus, who has become for us wisdom from God – that is, our righteousness [justification], holiness and [final] redemption' (*1 Cor. 1:30*). So sanctification is an essential link in the chain. To be in Christ is of necessity to have sanctification, which is as much a link in the chain as the other three. To miss sanctification is to miss Christ – and to miss Christ is to miss heaven. In the words of Thomas Watson, 'If God should justify a people and not sanctify them, He would justify a people whom He could not glorify.'

T. C. Hammond calls the attempt to separate justification from sanctification 'a most serious evil and may lead people to nourish an utterly false hope.' That is a polite way of saying that such people may well be what the Puritans called 'gospel hypocrites' on their way to hell. Said Ephraim Pagitt, 'Oh, it pleaseth nature well to have heaven and their lusts too' – but it cannot be done.[50] 'None can leap from Delilah's lap into Abraham's bosom.'

In the words of C. H. Spurgeon, 'Better a brief warfare and eternal rest than false peace and everlasting torment.'

[49]Kendall, R. T. *Op.cit.*, p. 100.
[50]Pagitt, Ephraim. *Op.cit.*, p. 88.

12: *Pure and Spotless*

It may be asked why holiness is necessary for salvation. If the Christian is justified by faith alone, and clothed in the righteousness of Christ Himself, why should he be required in addition to be holy in practice? Many answers might be given to this question.

First and foremost, as we have seen, one must argue that the very holiness of God Himself demands it. 'Be holy,' says God to His people – and gives the reason: 'because I am holy' (*1 Pet. 1:16*). The angels are ever conscious of this glorious attribute of God. Even though they have never sinned, they still veil their faces in God's holy presence. And they cry, 'Holy, holy, holy is the Lord Almighty; the whole earth is full of his glory' (*Isa. 6: 2–3*). And it is this thrice-holy God, whose eyes are too pure to behold evil or tolerate wrong (*Hab. 1:13*), who makes holiness a condition of entry into His presence.

Some inkling of this awesome holiness of God possessed the soul of the writer who penned the lines:

> Eternal Light! Eternal Light!
> How pure the soul must be,
> When, placed within Thy searching sight,
> It shrinks not, but with calm delight
> Can live and look on Thee.
>
> (*Thomas Binney*)

'How pure the soul must be!' God's essential holiness requires that the righteousness of Christ imputed to the

Christian in justification must also be imparted to him in sanctification. And this, indeed, is guaranteed in the new birth, for it is the inevitable desire of the born-again believer that he should be holy, as his Father is holy. It is a case of 'Like Father, like son'. God, who is holy, has no unholy children. Those who profess conversion but give no evidence of taking after the Holy Father are thereby proclaiming that they are not His sons at all. The true children of God are always holy, for 'without holiness no-one will see the Lord' (*Heb. 12:14*). The unholy shall not see His face. That privilege is reserved for the pure in heart (*Matt. 5:8*). It is for this reason, among others, that J. C. Ryle wrote, 'We must be saints on earth if ever we mean to be saints in heaven!'[51]

CHOSEN TO BE HOLY

A further argument for holiness may be seen in the fact that God elected us for this very purpose. 'He chose us in him [Christ] before the creation of the world to be holy and blameless in his sight' (*Eph. 1:4*). We were predestinated to be conformed to the image of Christ in all His spotless purity (*Rom. 8:29*). This divine choice makes it certain that we shall be like Him when He appears (*1 John 3:2*). From this fact, John deduces that everyone who has this hope in him purifies himself just as Christ is pure (*1 John 3:3*). His use of the word 'everyone' makes it quite certain that those who do not purify themselves will not see Christ, nor be like Him. By their lack of holiness they prove that they were not so predestinated. The apostle thus deals a crushing blow to Antinomianism.

PURCHASED SLAVES

One of the major incentives to holiness urged by Scripture

[51]Ryle, J. C. *Holiness* (1952), p. 46. James Clarke.

is the cross of our blessed Lord on Calvary's Hill. We are reminded repeatedly that His great object in dying was to purchase the slaves of sin and make them slaves of righteousness. Paul tells us that 'our great God and Saviour, Jesus Christ, gave himself for us to redeem us from all wickedness and to purify for himself a people that are his very own, eager to do what is good' (*Titus 2: 13–14*). 'He died for all,' says the same Apostle, 'that those who live should no longer live for themselves but for him who died for them and was raised again' (*2 Cor. 5:15*).

In fact, Christ went even beyond this. He intended in His death to purchase a bride whom He should one day marry – once He had purified her. 'Husbands, love your wives,' says Paul, just as Christ loved the church and gave himself up for her to make her holy, cleansing her by the washing with water through the word, and to present her to himself as a radiant church, without stain or wrinkle or any other blemish, but holy and blameless' (*Eph. 5:25–27*). John saw the bride on the eve of the wedding. By then the process of purification was complete. 'Fine linen, bright and clean, was given her to wear. (Fine linen stands for the righteous acts of the saints)' (*Rev. 19:8*). She had washed her robes 'and made them white in the blood of the Lamb' (*Rev. 7:14*).

Holiness is thus the debt of gratitude I owe to Him 'who loved me and gave himself for me' (*Gal. 2:20*). Did He tread alone the winepress of the fierceness and wrath of Almighty God, that I might not bear that wrath to all eternity? Was He forsaken by God that I might never be forsaken? Did He die that I might live? How then can I crucify Him afresh and put Him to an open shame? Out upon the suggestion! Sin becomes totally abhorrent and I flee it as I would the plague.

The stimulus to holiness that flows from the Cross has been the theme of some of the greatest hymns ever penned. Isaac Watts felt its force:

> When I survey the wondrous Cross
> On which the Prince of glory died,
> My richest gain I count but loss,
> And pour contempt on all my pride.

> Were the whole realm of nature mine,
> That were an offering far too small;
> Love so amazing, so divine,
> Demands my soul, my life, my all.

Perhaps, as Dr Lloyd-Jones said, Watts should have written:

> Love so amazing, so divine,
> Already has my soul, my life, my all.

For as a Christian I have no choice. All that I have and all I am are His – He has purchased my all with His blood. So Fergus Ferguson perhaps captured this truth better when he was constrained to write:

> He loved me and gave Himself for me,
> And surely I myself to Him will give;
> None, Jesus, will I ever love like Thee,
> And to Thy glory only will I live.

It is the inevitable biblical logic. Those who deduce from Calvary that they may live as they please align themselves with Satan. They may consequently expect to share his fate. 'Their condemnation,' says the apostle, 'is deserved' (*Rom. 3:8*).

EVERY BLESSING ARGUES HOLINESS

Every blessing of the Christian life argues holiness. Every good and perfect gift that I receive from the Father of the Heavenly Lights, every promise I take, every kindness I enjoy, tells me that God may reasonably expect me, in return, to live a holy life. This is the scriptural case. Note the Apostle Paul's deductive 'therefore'. In his Epistle to the Romans, after eleven chapters spent portraying God's mercies, he proceeds to argue, 'Therefore, I urge you, brothers, in view of God's mercy, to offer your bodies as living sacrifices, holy and pleasing to God – which is your spiritual worship. Do not conform any longer to the pattern of this world, but be transformed by the renewing of your mind. Then you will be able to test and approve what God's will is – his good, pleasing and perfect will' (*Rom. 12:1–2*).

The same pattern is discernible in the Epistle to the Ephesians. Immediately following three chapters on the riches of God's grace in Christ Jesus, the apostle draws the inevitable conclusion, 'As a prisoner for the Lord, then, I urge you to live a life worthy of the calling you have received. Be completely humble and gentle; be patient, bearing with one another in love. Make every effort to keep the unity of the Spirit through the bond of peace' (*Eph. 4:1–3*). The Letter to the Colossians, cast in the same mould, draws the same conclusion (*Col. 3:1ff*).

This means, in practice, that 'counting my blessings and naming them one by one', I proceed to live accordingly. The argument, simply stated, runs something like this. Did God love from all eternity a guilty worm like me? Then I will show my love in return by leading a life of likeness to Jesus. Did He call me by His grace, give me life when I was dead, sight when blind, healing when lame, hearing when deaf? Has He justified me, adopted me, united me to Christ? Is He sanctifying me, guiding me, providing for my every need? Will He one day glorify me? If so, then I will raise a paean of praise from my redeemed heart – and live a life whose purity brings glory to God.

Listen to the saintly Edward Payson, who put it all so lyrically as he lay on his death bed awaiting the day when he should see His Lord face to face and never, never sin:

'What an assemblage of motives to holiness does the gospel present! I am a Christian. What then? Why, I am a redeemed sinner, a pardoned rebel, all through grace, and by the most wonderful means which infinite wisdom could devise. I am a Christian. What then? Why, I am a temple of God; and surely I ought to be pure and holy. I am a Christian. What then? I am a child of God and ought to be filled with filial love, reverence, joy and gratitude. I am a Christian. What then? Why, I am a disciple of Christ and must imitate Him who was meek and lowly in heart, and pleased not himself. I am a Christian. What then? Why, I am an heir of heaven, and hastening on to the abodes of the blessed, to join the full choir of the glorified ones in singing the song of Moses and of the Lamb; and surely I ought to learn that song on earth.'[52]

Small wonder that Stephen Tyng commented on that testimony, 'How can man make void the law by his love for sin, who is in possession of such privileges as these?'

GOOD WORKS

Our Lord Himself indicates a further reason why His people should produce good works, namely, the glory which they bring to God the Father. 'Let your light shine before men,' He says, 'that they may see your good deeds and praise your Father in heaven' (*Matt. 5:16*). Peter makes the same point. He asserts that seeing Christians' good deeds causes pagans to 'glorify God on the day he visits us' (*1 Pet. 2:12*). There is no higher motive than this. The glory of God is the chief desire of the Son, as it is of the holy angels. And grace has made it the prime aim of the believer.

[52]Payson, Edward. Quoted in Tyng, Stephen H. *Lectures on the Law and the Gospel* (1867), p. 181. Grant.

We note here, for the last time, the importance which the Bible places on works as evidence of God's grace in the life. A mere profession is not enough. 'Grace that cannot be seen is no grace at all' (Ryle). Unbelievers are not really interested in a man's profession of faith, though it be couched in the most eloquent theological language. But they are impressed by what a man is and does. As the popular proverb has it, 'Actions speak louder than words'. This is basically what James is saying in the second chapter of his Epistle. Profession of faith is easy. But the only way to decide whether it is genuine or not is by its works. A faith without works is, quite simply, bogus.

Our Lord spoke of those who made an empty profession of faith. 'Lord, Lord,' they cried with the greatest piety, but they did not heed His call to holiness (*Luke 6:46*).

D. L. Moody knew the situation only too well. No doubt he had grown tired of hearing countless professions of faith from those whose lives remained unchanged. He expressed his reaction to all that in his own picturesque way. 'It is a great deal better to live a holy life than to talk about it. Lighthouses do not ring bells and fire cannon to call attention to their shining – they just shine!'

CHRIST'S SECOND COMING

The Apostle John says that the thought of Christ's Second Coming is itself an incentive to holiness. 'Dear friends,' he writes, 'we know that when he appears, we shall be like him, for we shall see him as he is. Everyone who has this hope in him purifies himself, just as he is pure' (*I John 3:2–3*). The Apostle Peter develops the same theme. 'Since everything will be destroyed in this way, what kind of people ought you to be? You ought to live holy and godly lives as you look forward to the day of God . . . So then, dear friends, since you are looking forward to this, make every effort to be found spotless, blameless and at peace with him' (*2 Pet. 3:11–14*).

The Apostle Paul urges the same consideration on his Roman readers. 'The hour has come for you to wake up from your slumber, because our salvation is nearer now than when we first believed. The night is nearly over; the day is almost here. So let us put aside the deeds of darkness and put on the armour of light. Let us behave decently, as in the daytime, not in orgies and drunkenness, not in sexual immorality and debauchery, not in dissension and jealousy. Rather, clothe yourselves with the Lord Jesus Christ, and do not think about how to gratify the desires of the sinful nature' (*Rom. 13:11–14*).

HEAVEN

Finally, contemplation of 'that land of pure delight, where saints immortal reign' acts as a spur to a life of holiness here below. It must do so, for we know that nothing impure can ever enter God's heaven.

> There is a city bright;
> Closed are its gates to sin;
> Nought that defileth,
> Nought that defileth
> Can ever enter in.
>
> (*Mary A. S. Deck*)

There we shall set eyes on the One of unsullied purity, who is 'holy, blameless, pure, set apart from siners.' The only angels there will be the holy ones who kept their first estate. The only people there will be those who have been purged from every stain of sin. The dogs, the magicians, the sexually immoral, the murderers, the idolaters, the liars will all be excluded – for ever (*Rev. 22:14–15*).

[94]

So all those on earth who are destined to pass through those gates of pearly splendour have already begun to purify themselves from everything that contaminates body and spirit and to perfect holiness out of reverence for God. Their heart cry is that of Charles Wesley:

> Finish then Thy new creation,
> Pure and spotless let us be;
> Let us see Thy great salvation
> Perfectly restored in Thee;
> Changed from glory into glory,
> Till in heaven we take our place,
> Till we cast our crowns before Thee,
> Lost in wonder, love and praise.

APPENDIX

CALVIN AND URSINUS ON JUSTIFICATION AND GOOD WORKS

Calvin in *Institutes* III, xviii, 1, explains the relation of the believer's good works to his justification as follows: 'The declaration that God will render to everyone according to his works is easily explained. For that phrase indicates the *order* of events rather than the *cause* of them. It is beyond all doubt that the Lord proceeds to the consummation of our salvation by these gradations of mercy: "Whom he hath predestinated them he calls; whom he hath called he justifies; and whom he hath justified he finally glorifies" (*Rom. 8:30*). Though he receives his children into eternal life of his mere mercy, yet since he conducts them to the possession of it through a course of good works that he may fulfil his work in them in the order he has appointed, we need not wonder if they are said to be rewarded according to their works, by which they are prepared to receive the crown of immortality. And for this reason they are properly said to "work out their own salvation," while, devoting themselves to good works, they aspire to eternal life. Whence it appears that the word *work* is not opposed to grace, but refers to human endeavours; and therefore it does not follow either that believers are the authors of their own salvation, or that salvation proceeds from their works. By their good works they prove themselves to be the genuine children of God, by their resemblance to their heavenly Father in righteousness and holiness.'

Ursinus (*Christian Religion*, Q.52) thus explains Christ's reference to the works of the believer in the day of judgment: 'It is *objected* that unto every man shall be given according to his works: therefore judgment shall be given to all, not according to the gospel, but according to the doctrine of the law. *Answer:* In this sense it shall be given unto the elect according to their works; not that their works are merits, but in that they are the effects of faith. Wherefore, then, unto the elect shall be given according to their works; that is, they shall be judged according to the effects of faith; and to be judged according to faith is to be judged according to the gospel. Now Christ shall rather judge according to works as the effects of faith, than according to faith as their cause: I. Because he will have it known to others why he so judgeth, lest the ungodly and condemned persons might object that he giveth us eternal life unjustly. He will prove by our works the fruits of our faith, that our faith was sincere and true, and therefore we are such as those to whom life is due according to the promise. Wherefore he will show them our works and will bring them forth as testimonies to refute them, that we have in this life applied unto us Christ's merit. 2. That we may have comfort in this life, that we shall hereafter, according to our works, stand at his right hand.'

A DANGEROUS IMBALANCE

There is also another series of once popular and widely circulated devotional and theological works, but now forgotten, or nearly so, amidst the multitude of more modern ones that have superseded them in public favour, to which I would for a moment allude, I mean Romaine's *Life*, *Walk*, and *Triumph of Faith*. Of these works it may be said, they are each the reproduction of the other, and all three are books of one idea – but that one how great and glorious – 'CHRIST IS ALL:' or put in another form, 'THE LORD OUR RIGHTEOUSNESS.' With what delight the intelligent and devout believer, whose creed and whose heart are replete with *Christology*, may and must read these works, I need not say; but he must be an *intelligent* and *devout* believer to do so. He must be like their author, so entirely in the holy spell and fascination of the cross of Christ, as to be able to look at nothing else. This *was* the case with Romaine: he so constantly walked and basked in the noontide glory of the Sun of Righteousness, that he had eyes for no other object. He was so engrossed with the great orb of gospel light, that he saw not even the wide and glowing landscape of beauty which that Sun revealed and illuminated. *His* faith was only or chiefly faith in Christ for *justification*. He shut up his readers to faith, and shut up that faith to Christ. It was a noble seclusion I admit, and yet it may be doubted whether it was a scriptural one. Christ is the centre of the Christian scheme, but there is also a circumference; and a true faith, while it begins at the centre, does not stop there, but radiates through all the intermediate spaces to the outer circle. Romaine's works, spiritual, evangelical, and experimental as they are, must be considered by every judicious mind as defective, – they are not a fair impress of the New Testament as a whole: there is, if not too much of Paul, too little of James; if not too much of the Epistle to the Galatians, too little of the Sermon upon the Mount. Or to give another illustration, he dwelt almost exclusively on the justifying faith of the Epistle to the Romans, without taking up either the justifying works of the Epistle of James, or the general faith of the eleventh chapter of the Epistle to the Hebrews. What was the consequence? Just what might have been expected: he prepared the way for theoretic Antinomianism, and many of his hearers when he died became the admirers and followers of that notorious personification of spiritual pride, presumption, and arrogance, William Huntington. For what *is* Antinomianism? The gospel abstracted from the law and resting upon a basis of sovereign mercy, instead of being founded upon the principles of moral government – a scheme intended to subvert the law, while mercy is exercised towards its offenders. A true faith therefore, must be exercised as much towards all the duties of the law as towards all the blessings of the gospel.

John Angell James in
The Course of Faith, or
The Practical Believer Delineated,
2nd edit., 1857, pp. vii–viii.

THOMAS ROBINSON TO ROBERT HALL ON ANTINOMIANISM
Leicester, Dec. 22, 1787.

MY DEAR SIR,

I am sorry to hear of your alarm about Antinomianism; but hope it will not spread, as your fears might suggest. Had I thought you unprepared to resist such an attack upon your most holy faith, I should have endeavoured to have furnished you with a few weapons. But, I doubt not, the Lord will enable you to defend his truth, and guard it against all dangerous perversions and abuse. In a few words, I would observe, that the system of Antinomianism sets aside half the work of Christ, and the chief part of the operations of the Spirit, and leaves us where it found us, the slaves of sin utterly unchanged. It puts a forced and most unnatural construction on all those passages which speak of holiness and good works; and keeps out of sight, or rather denies, the grand design of redemption, viz., to bring us back to God, by making us submit to his government. If the law be no rule of life, why does Paul talk of it, and show what is contained in it? Why does he declare that he is not without law to God, but under the law to Christ? But I will not multiply passages on so plain a point. I will only observe, that the law of God is no other than a transcript of his most holy mind, and that whoever loves one must love the other. God is also unchangeable in his mind, and, therefore, his moral law, (which is only the declaration of his will respecting the conduct of his rational creatures) cannot be repealed . . .

From *The Fathers and Founders of the
London Missionary Society*,
John Morrison, vol. 2, p. 97.

WORKS AND FUTURE GLORY

'By patience in well-doing.' Perhaps Meyer's comment is as close as any to the thought expressed, that this 'contains the standard, the regulative principle, by which the seeking after glory . . . is guided'. The word rendered 'patience' is perhaps better translated by 'perseverance' or 'endurance'. We are reminded of the truth that it is he who endures to the end that will be saved (*Matt. 24:13*) and that 'we are made partakers of Christ, if we hold fast the beginning of our confidence firm unto the end' (*Heb. 3:14;* cf. *Col. 1:22,23*). The complementation of perseverance in well-doing and the aspiration of hope underlines the lesson that these may never be separated. Works without redemptive aspiration are dead works. Aspiration without good works is presumption.

John Murray on Romans 2:7

In reference to the precise question, the judgment of believers, certain positions need to be set forth. (1) The distinction between judgment according to works and salvation on account of works needs to be fully appreciated. The latter is entirely contrary to the gospel Paul preached, is not implied in judgment according to works, and is that against which the burden of this Epistle is directed. Paul does not even speak of judgment *on account of works* in reference to believers. (2) Believers are justified by faith *alone* and they are saved by grace *alone*. But two qualifications need to be added to these propositions. (a) They are never justified by a faith that is alone. (b) In salvation we must not so emphasise grace that we overlook the salvation itself. The concept of salvation involves what we are saved *to* as well as what we are saved *from*. We are saved to holiness and good works (cf. *Eph. 2:10*). And holiness manifests itself in good works. (3) The judgment of God must have respect to the person in the full extent of his relationship and must therefore take into account the fruits in which salvation issues and which constitute the saved condition. It is not to faith or justification in abstraction that God's judgment will have respect but to these in proper relationship to the sum-total of elements comprising a saved state. (4) The criterion of good works is the law of God and the law of God is not abrogated for the believer. He is not without law to God; he is under law to Christ (cf. *I Cor. 9:21* and see comments on *6:14*). The judgment of God would not be according to truth if the good works of believers were ignored. (5) Good works as the evidences of faith and of salvation by grace are therefore the criteria of judgment and to suppose that the principle, 'who will render to every man according to his works' (*vs. 6*), has no relevance to the believer would be to exclude good works from the indispensable place which they occupy in the biblical doctrine of salvation.

> John Murray summarising the teaching of
> Romans 2:5–16 in *The Epistle to the Romans*,
> The English Text with Introduction, Exposition
> and Notes, vol 1, 1960.

THE EVIDENCE OF SANCTIFICATION

Believers, even in the times and under the dispensation of the gospel, are not to lay aside or cast off Scripture marks, signs, or evidences grounded upon sanctification and holiness, in order to the finding out of their spiritual state and condition. For wherefore doth the Spirit of God here thus characterise persons 'in Christ' *which walk not after the flesh, but after the Spirit,* but for this end, that by this character or mark men may know whether they be indeed in Christ or not; the like you find in very many other places. The Antinomians do not approve of this doctrine; they will not hear of any evidences or signs of this or that privilege, fetched from sanctification or holiness, or anything inherent in ourselves; an opinion weak and false, yea, directly contrary to the tenor of the Word. How great a part of the Bible might be blotted out, as altogether useless, if what they affirm herein was true. Read but the first Epistle of John, you will find it throughout to be characteristical or evidential of men's state from the fruits and effects of sanctification; the places therein are so many and so common, that I neither well can, nor do I in the least need to make any particular rehearsal of them. It is strange that men cannot distinguish betwixt grounds as to the thing, and evidences as to the person. Far be it from us to make sanctification or holy walking the grounds of our union with Christ, or of our justification; yet they are the evidences by which we come to know that we are in Christ and justified by him. And the question is not what the Spirit of God can do, or possibly sometimes may do, viz., whether he doth not in an immediate manner, without the making use of these signs, reveal to a believer his union with Christ, and interest in gospel-blessings; but the question is, What is the ordinary method of the Spirit in the witnessing and clearing up of these things to a soul? And surely that is the first by the witnessing of faith, sincerity, holiness of life, and then by witnessing to them and upon them. And a Christian cannot ordinarily expect assurance of his union with Christ, or of any other thing, but in this mediate way.

Thomas Jacomb (died 1687) on Romans 8:1
Sermons on the Eighth Chapter of the Epistle to the Romans,
1868 Nichol reprint, p. 77.

'Let it never be forgotten that, though we preach faith, faith, faith as the great means of salvation, yet we never say that you are saved unless there is a change wrought in you, and good works are produced in you; for "faith without works is dead, being alone." Faith saves, but it is the faith which causes men to do well; and if there be a faith (and there is such a faith) which leaves a man just what he was, and permits him to indulge in sin, it is the faith of devils . . .'

C. H. Spurgeon, *Metropolitan Tabernacle Pulpit*, vol 27, 1881. pp. 681–2.

Index